ALTO SAX TO WINTER BEAVERS

Vignettes of Life from 1946 to 2004

by

Charles (Chuck) Wallace

authorHOUSE™

1663 LIBERTY DRIVE, SUITE 200
BLOOMINGTON, INDIANA 47403
(800) 839-8640
WWW.AUTHORHOUSE.COM

First published by AuthorHouse 07/20/05

ISBN: 1-4208-4047-9 (e)
ISBN: 1-4208-4088-6 (sc)

Printed in the United States of America
Bloomington, Indiana

This book is printed on acid-free paper.

Table of Contents

ALTO SAX TO WINTER BEAVERS

VIGNETTES FROM 1946 TO 2004

Alto Sax – Chuck will substitute for a sick sax-man in the Phil Harris Band, at the Fairmont Hotel in San Francisco. Can he get on with a big band?

Any Luck – A fly fisherman is asked about his success as a fisherman.

A Real Drag – He hooked a big trout, but his reel of 20 years fails him. Can he land the fish?

Salmon Poachers – Who or what removed the biggest fish of the day?

Sanctuary – He spots that mammoth trout on the last hour of the last day of vacation. Can he recover?

Country Justice – In a small town, the Lay Leader of the church is accused of being too drunk to go home for three nights. How can he and his wife dispel these rumors?

Christmas Spirit – His daughter came home from college to be with Dad. His lady friend controls a foundation which helps young artists. She asked his daughter to apply. A trip to travel and study in Italy is the grant. Will she use it to advantage? Or marry the Italian artist who proposed?

Homecoming – Two brothers love the same girl. Younger man enlists and goes to Viet Nam. Older man stays home, makes lots of money and marries the girl. Young brother returns. After a brief confrontation, one of them is dead.

Oh Ye of Little Faith – A Hospice volunteer meets her new client. He falls in love with her, but she maintains her distance. After his death, generous gifts are made to the former volunteer and his daughter in Italy.

Our Big Break – Three college students, while playing a freebie, are offered a job for a big dinner dance. Get two more musicians and a vocalist. Can they succeed?

Reply C/O Red Cross – A woman volunteer came into the staff lounge where a single "swabbie" was relaxing. She was an officer's wife and the Navy prohibited personal contact between the two. They fell in love and faced many obstacles to their relationship. Can love conquer all?

* **"C" for Courage** – The author's daughter was hit head-on in an automobile accident which left her near death. See how the family responds, or doesn't?

* A true story

Winter Beavers – Grandpa beaver hasn't prepared for winter. His wife locks him out of their den. What to do?

Preface

1946 – World War II had ended and all the world wanted to get back to peace. The period till 2004 was far from peaceful, marred by the assination of President Kennedy, the impeachment of President Nixon and the murder of Attorney General Robert Kennedy.

Russia entered space travel before the U.S. did. Congress reacted by ordering public schools to teach more math, science and foreign language. This caused considerable confusion among educators and parents.

Military actions included Viet Nam, Korea and Desert Storm. Recently we obliterated Afghanistan and are still entangled in a mess called Iraq.

These stories make no attempt to deal directly with the above mentioned events, rather how a middle class family survived.

Your author was a high school teacher, administrator and college professor, hoping to give three wonderful daughters an education suitable for their time.

Comments or questions are welcome.

Charles (Chuck) Wallace

ALTO SAX

His call came before the sun was up, "Chuck, get your ass outta the sack! This is the big break you've been waiting for."

"Louie, you crazy son-of-a-bitch, it's the middle of the night."

"I waited to call. It's 6:00 a.m. Listen up. Get your sax and tux. You're sitting in with me tonight at the Fairmont."

"Louie, I'm in no condition for one of your sick jokes; wife's on a rampage, the kid has been down with the measles."

He cut in, "No joke. You're gonna be the alto sax man with Phil Harris tonight. Our man is in the hospital. I told Phil I knew a good man, played with him in Guam. Navy ships came from all over the Pacific to hear us."

"No bull? When do I check in?"

"Call me about 2:00 o'clock this afternoon. Now, don't let me down. My ass is way out there for you on this one."

"Gottcha. And, Louie, thanks, I owe you…"

"Buddy, you saved me, out there."

Thank God, I took my discharge pay and had my sax completely overhauled: cleaned, new pads and even resilvered. Alice was screaming about all the bills, and how we needed a larger apartment.

I've had gigs, some good bands and some little ones but never got the break I needed to hit the road with a name band.

Somehow we managed to survive, these last three years. Now Carol was two years old and Alice has just about convinced me to use my G.I. benefits and go back to college. Out there in the Pacific my sax kept me from going "over-the-hill" many times.

When I told Alice about the job, she almost cried. "Just one more excuse for not making the decision." Dejectedly she said, "I'm going shopping. You get to take care of Carol this morning."

I got my sax and jammed away. Carol was on the floor playing with some gray modeling clay. She pulled on my pants, wanting me to look at her, "Da...Da." I was lost in my dream of the big time. She smashed the modeling clay, climbed up on my lap, and pushed so hard on the sax I had to stop playing. Blue eyes scolded, "No...no."

Alice got back later than I'd expected. I had to rent a tux, borrow some black shoes and clear with the Union. I got to the Fairmont a half hour early and Louie checked me out on their numbers.

I sat at the end of the front row, Louie and two other sax players were to my left. I felt I was as good as they were during the first set. When Phil Harris started "That's What I Like About the South," an electric shock went through the place. Everyone in the audience stood and broke into applause. The band came alive with new energy that left me far behind. When he finished, the applause nearly brought the roof down.

I was nervous as hell! I realized the best players were far better than anyone I'd ever worked with, but felt I could keep up with two of the sax players.

The good news was that the piano player, the most experienced member of the band and did most of their arrangements, gave me "thumbs up" when I stood for a six bar break. But, I was having trouble. I couldn't keep the sax in tune. I'd be flat sometimes and it never sounded right.

After we finished the early show, the trombone player in back of me called, "Hey, stupid. What did you do with the money?"

"What money?" I replied.

"The money your mother gave you for lessons."

Louie told me, "Pack it up. Don't ever let me see you again."

I stopped for a beer. My friend Dexter bought one for me.

"All dressed for a party, but by the way you look, I'd guess you screwed up. Right?"

"I played in the Phil Harris band, one very short performance. Yeah, I blew my big chance."

When I crawled into bed, I told Alice, "I'll enroll tomorrow. I'll never make it as a sax man."

Her kiss was the warmest and the longest since I'd known her. "Sax man, NO. Sex man, YES!"

The following day I took my sax to my favorite shop. It took the repairman a few minutes to find the problem. "Chuck, there's a wad of modeling clay in the neck of your sax."

The author expresses appreciation to Chuck Lavaroni, an accomplished alto sax player and leader of his own band in Marin County, California, for some of the ideas contained in this story.

"ANY LUCK?"

A heavy masculine voice carried half way across Manzanita Lake, "Any Luck?" I was about ten feet from shore, hunkered over in intense concentration, focused on a trout which had just taken something from the film without breaking the surface.

I turned to face a forty-something man, surrounded by a wife and three daughters.

"Luck?" I asked, "standing in this crystal clear lake, looking up at that magnificent spectacle, Mount Lassen, with a clear blue sky and warm sun, I'm one of the luckiest men in the world.

"You wondered, have I caught any fish today? Just a minute ago, I hooked and played a powerful trout. When he was tired, I brought him close, knelt down to twist the fly loose, then held him for a moment to admire the brilliant colors and strength of the fragile body. You made a good fight of it. Now, go back home where you belong."

The man led his family off to see the rest of the Park. I was certain that he didn't have the faintest idea about what I'd just said.

A REAL DRAG

On the second cast after lunch I had a solid hit. Water erupted as if a nuclear missile had been launched from a submarine and a big beautiful rainbow trout cleared the surface by more than a foot, shaking his head and arching his body in an explosive fight to free the hook dangling from his lip.

He fell back with a loud splash - then headed downstream with the force and speed of a torpedo.

It was the third day after Christmas and several fly fishermen were trying their new gear in the impoundment below Lost Creek Dam which we call the "Holy Water." This section of the Rogue River has an excellent food supply so some fish achieve rapid growth and put on more weight per inch than in the open river. I was in the lower section where we face the bank, made medium to short casts, slightly upstream and let the line make a full arc as it goes downstream.

The spirited fight of my fish took him into deep water, leading to the outlet at the end of the impoundment when he suddenly stopped. He saw the large yellow warning sign, "Danger, Dam Ahead" posted for such errant beings.

Unfortunately for me, my faithful reel that had served me well for at least twenty years took that critical moment to lose the drag. Fly line went everywhere. It looped over the handle of the reel, a big loop managed to get around the butt of the fly rod, and many smaller loops stuck out dangerously from every gap in the body of the reel.

One of the most experienced fishermen in our club was on the bank so close that I could have easily snagged him with a short cast. "Keep your rod up! Don't give him any slack!" Dave shouted

He'd told the club, when he was a small boy his dad took him into the woods where they were logging to yell "timber" when a tree was felled. He certainly had the voice for it.

Somehow I managed to release the catch on the spool and free it from the reel. I dropped the spool into the pouch inside my chest waders.

The fish jumped out of the water, not quite as high as before and with a little less action than before and decided he'd rejoin his buddies in the lake above the dam. He headed directly at me on his way upstream. I held the fly rod high above my head with my left hand and retrieved line as best I could with my right. Of course, as the fish approached, line was all around me on the surface in and around both legs so I didn't dare move.

Dave was now yelling, "Take up the slack. You'll lose him!"

As my adversary came directly at me, not more than three feet away, a big loop of fly line formed a circle and that fish came out of the water inside the circle then fell back again. I was sure he'd made a knot with his acrobatics. Somehow he kept going and I recovered enough line to clear the loop.

Dave began to laugh. I'm sure it looked like "Chinese fire drill" to an experienced fisherman, but I was so excited about the possibility of landing that beautiful specimen that I couldn't enjoy the ludicrous situation.

In order for the fish to leave the small section of river where we met, he had to go over a gravel bar which barely had two inches of water. He took out line and circled, swirled and came out of the water again, then headed into deeper water. By now I'd regained most of the drifting line and tucked it into the pouch with the spool.

It settled into a more conventional battle. With my left hand around the fly rod I controlled the pressure on the line and with my right hand I played line out or recovered it. That fish swirled, dove, and surfaced nearly ten more minutes.

When he seemed to be tired, I worked him toward me. He saw my legs and with a final burst of power, left the shallow water and headed back one more time.

"Get your landing net, or you'll lose him!" Dave yelled.

My net was attached to a ring at the neck, in back of my fly vest. I bent over to let it fall by my side, and the errant spool with all the extra fly line fell into the water.

Believe it or not, that fish came into my net on the first swoop. He was more that twenty inches of the brightest, most brilliant crimson streaked rainbow trout that I've ever taken.

With a twist of my wrist, the barbless hook was out his mouth and he headed back to his deep water home.

Dave led the cheers of the other fly fishermen who'd watched the show.

When I took the reel into my favorite fly shop, Paul determined that, "Chuck, the fingers on that drag had just worn enough for them to miss engaging the sprocket of the spool."

I grumbled, "They just don't make 'em like they used to. That's only gone a hundred thousand miles."

SALMON POACHERS

He was a big man, dressed in military fatigues with polished maroon ankle top boots. He extended a thick, stubby-fingered right hand. "Call me Doc. Name's Delbert, but even my best friends don't dare use that."

"I'm Chuck." I chanced putting my slender hand in his vice, and quickly withdrew it before it was mutilated.

Our guide, Gary, was waiting in the drift boat. He called, "Come on Colonel Doc, you've missed the early morning bite." Looking at me, "You must be Chuck." The disapproving tone of voice made it clear that he considered it an insult that a city fellow in Levi's and rubber boots would tag along.

"Yeah, glad you could take me."

Gary asked, "You ever fished salmon before?"

"No. Mostly ocean fishing." I stowed my gear.

Gary explained, "Colonel Doc is in charge of the hospital at the Presidio. He served in Europe, and the South Pacific during WWII. He's been around the world."

Obviously, Gary was proud to have him in his boat.

Doc carefully transferred a large wicker basket from his Bronco to Gary, who was standing in the boat. "Easy Boy, some of the finest brie in France is in there for our lunch."

We fished 'till noon without touching a salmon, then pulled out at a sandy cove. Doc said, "By God, we'll eat even if we can't find a fish." He laid out a red and white checked tablecloth, then brought brie, two bowls of dips and small nachos for appetizers. The wine was a French Burgundy that was like velvet. Doc cut French rolls and layered prime rib with Swiss cheese on them. Small French pastries were served as dessert. We had hot coffee spiked with brandy after dessert.

I told Doc, "I've been to France, but I never had a lunch to equal this. Thanks."

In the first hole after lunch, Doc had a good strike. He reared back with a mighty jerk, and the hook came flying above our heads into the water beyond the stern of the boat. My mouth instinctively opened to offer a suggestion about the way to set a hook. One look at Doc cut that idea short.

It was after four o'clock when we came to a deep hole with a big eddy. Gary positioned the boat so we would drift the bait along the outer edge of the sweep. We changed to full ounce weights and put fresh roe on. With the first bounce of the weight on the bottom, I had a solid hit, raised the pole and called, "fish on!"

My pole bent straight down as line spun out of the reel. The boat rolled perilously when I stood to work my fish, pumping and reeling just like I would for a big halibut. The fish pulled around the bow and I yelled for Doc, "Get your line out of the way."

As he swung his pole toward the stern, he replied, "Dammit, man. Handle your fish. I'll get one on the next swing."

Fortunately, the trouble maker went back toward my side. After twenty minutes, I worked it to the surface where Gary netted a salmon.

"Good work, Chuck. You've fished somewhere before. That'll go twenty six pounds." I thought that was the highest compliment he could give, without irritating Doc.

Doc's comment was, "Gary, go find one a pound bigger or we'll stay out 'till you do."

In a few minutes Doc had a bite. He raised his pole firmly, and was into a good fish. Gary anchored the boat and I pulled my line in.

Doc was pumping and reeling, "You found one a lot heavier than Chuck's. I can hardly move this sucker." When the fish broke the surface, Gary and I agreed.

It turned and went down again, then all at once the line went slack.

Doc was shocked. "I didn't do anything, he just got off." He brought his line in and examined the rig. Gary offered, "Must not have been hooked solid, it just came off."

Doc looked at me as though it was my fault he didn't set the hook in his usual way.

As Gary was pulling the anchor for us to leave, he saw them. "Damn poachers. Look Doc, those two otters stole your salmon right off the hook."

It was the funniest sight I ever saw. Two small fresh water otters, no more than three pounds each and about a foot long, were struggling with a much too big salmon which had lots of fight left in it. They were dragging it along the rocks, first one then the other holding the fish by the head, trying to get it to their den on the far bank.

"Pull over to shore and I'll kill those bastards with my bare hands." Doc yelled.

Gary just kept rowing for home.

SANCTUARY

It was still dark, but the last slice of moon shed enough light for me to scramble through the brush.

I'd returned to this lava rock field at the foot of Mount Shasta after nearly a year of preparation. In just a few minutes, I would know victory or retreat in defeat.

The stillness of the forest in those last moments of night, just before the beginning of a new day, provided an appropriate setting for the encounter. Every thorny bush and berry vine protested my passing by grabbing and tearing at my waders.

As soon as I heard the muted song of the rifle that I'd come to know so well, I hunkered down and moved in a duck-waddle for the last ten yards. I wedged my body around and through the matted underbrush to the big rock overlook rendezvous point. I crawled the last few feet on elbows and knees.

When I'd slithered to the upstream side of the big rock at the head of the pool, I strained to hear the distinctive "slurp" of my adversary sucking in his daily meal.

"The World in Solemn Stillness Lay" flashed into my consciousness.

Knees and elbows screeching their objections, I stilled my breathing to hear the faintest break in the music of the rifle above the deep, dark, lava-lined pool.

Last year I had watched the movements of the brute for three days, studying his habits until I was ready. At the last moment of dusk, I had floated my "exact imitation" of the latest hatch down between two shiny rocks. He rose to inspect it, then flipped it with his tail as though he were insulted. I had retreated that day knowing full well that I would return another time to do battle with the "King of the McCloud River."

Two years earlier, I had come upon this bull rainbow in his lair on the last evening of my precious week's vacation. My best casts didn't even draw a response from him.

The first delicate pink glow of daylight brought the peak of Mount Shasta afire. Now I could make out the shrubs and oak trees on the opposite side of the pool.

Then it started! The slurp-pause, slurp, slurp of feeding trout. But those were just pre-adolescent smaller fish.

A louder, basso-profoundo "slurp." That's him!

I cautiously unfurled my leader and tippet from the pole. Sheltered by the huge lava rock, I quietly worked the line through the guides to extend six inches beyond the rod tip. I crouched, half-lifted an arm and deftly flipped the fly to the white rock in the neck of the pool that I'd selected for my target. After the line fed evenly through the guides, I pulled back gently to clear the belly of the line free of any slack.

Coached by experts not to stand, I continued to crouch, concentrating every ounce of energy on that floating line.

The splash of his hit, and the force of his blow, came all at once. The reel whirred that greatest of all songs, zzzzzzzzzing!

Instinct took over as I jumped to my feet and held the fly rod high over my head. With his first leap, near the head of the pool, he cleared the water by several inches. How could my angel-hair tippet possibly withstand such force!

The reel sang loud and clear as he ran the full length of that thirty foot pool. With his next move, he rose more than a foot above the water. I couldn't believe that my fly was still in his lip. The heavy splash when he came down sounded like a log thrown into the water.

He dove deep into his fortress in the rocks and paused there, sulking. I kept light tension on the line, expecting him to make a break out through the rocks at the tail of the pool. Instead, he leapt again, twice, only this time his leaps were noticeably shorter and less vigorous.

More than ten minutes he twisted, swirled and splashed, then as he tired, I drew him toward the rocky bank. He saw he was in trouble and with a mighty surge of power flung his body back into the deepest part of the pool.

My fly rod was in an arc, the tip level with the reel when he made his next move.

Freedom waited beyond the outlet of the pool and that was his destination. The drag on the reel allowed him to take the line, but at a high price. He stopped short of the outlet and stayed in deep water under the protection of a rock ledge.

Gradually, I gained line. I moved to a more favorable landing position and applied pressure.

Finally, he was exhausted and in my hands at the edge of the pool.

More than twenty inches long, he weighed at least five pounds. His silver sides reflected the brilliance of the sky, and the distinctive scarlet red stripe running the full length of his body was the brightest I'd ever seen on a rainbow trout. As I held my hands under him and grasped the barbless hook in my fingers, I paused...

I have knelt in reverence in Notre Dame Cathedral and stood in admiration as I gazed up into the Sistine Chapel, but for this fisherman, that moment with a magnificent quivering body in my hands at the foot of Mount Shasta, brought a greater communion with our Creator than any other experience I have ever had.

I freed the fly with a twist of the wrist. A momentary movement of his body to get the water over his gills, and he groggily retuned to reign over his kingdom.

This fly fishermen returned to his world of work with a vivid image of the noblest sanctuary in all the world.

COUNTRY JUSTICE

Seems like as soon as the new year comes around, the tax forms come in the mail. The I.R.S. wants all my money, and they want it first. Well, the day I was in the post office and got my tax forms, Josie motioned for me to come to the counter, she had to tell me somethin'. Usually that means some family in the valley needs help, clothes or food, and me bein' Lay Leader of the Church and an officer in the Grange, I know ways to get help for 'em from folks who'll be glad to do it.

Not like her usual self, Josie fidgeted and dropped a bundle of junk mail, then turned to see me. Her face was white and she never looked in my eyes. "Edgar" she said so low I could barely hear her, "Guess I'm the only one in the valley could tell you... and I can't believe it myself, but I've heard it from two families, so you'd better know."

"Josie, for goodness sake, we've known each other like brother and sister for years, say your piece and get it over."

"They said that your drinking problem has gotten much worse, in fact it was so bad that you were too drunk to go home three nights last week... there now, I've said what I heard."

"Heard! Josie you know damn well I don't ever drink enough to get drunk. An' as for stayin' out three nights... Emily wouldn't let me back in the house if I stayed out one night, an' as for three... I wouldn't be standin' here worrin' about taxes, that's for damn sure!" I stomped outta that post office madder than I'd been since Nixon was re-elected.

I knew I couldn't work, though the high school where I'm care-taker is just across the street from the post office, so I tucked the tax forms inside my shirt and got on my bicycle to cool off while I was goin' home.

After forty years of marriage to me, Emily stays calm when I come inside the house with a real mad-on. She was in the kitchen puttin' the morning dishes away, smiled as I came through the door as if she'd greeted me that time in the morning every day of our married life.

I stomped around the dining room, threw my hat into the big chair in the parlor and generally made a fool of myself tryin' to calm down. Emily came through the swingin' door between the kitchen and dining room with a pitcher of cool milk and some muffins she'd saved from a church dinner.

Sure is wonderful how a smile and gentle hand-holding takes the fire outta a nasty nettle sting or a real mad-on.

She wouldn't hear my story 'till we'd had some milk and a muf-fin. "Now, it must be something worse than taxes that brought you home." Emily said,

After I told her what Josie said, she just sat back in her chair and played with some crumbs left from the muffin.

"Who'd want your job at the school?" she asked.

"I know right off five men who are outta work and think they'd be better 'n me, say I'm too old."

"You'd lose your job, wouldn't you if you'd done those things?" Emily was concerned.

"Faster than a crooked politician." Then I thought a bit, "Especially if one of those men has a relative on the board of trustees."

Emily was still quiet, like she was doin' her own thinkin', "Who wants to be a Lay Leader... besides Josie Perkins who has been passed over twice!" She spoke slowly and deliberately.

"I'd plum forgot that Josie tried to be Lay Leader. First time she didn't pass the exams about the Bible, then later the congregation didn't approve her... most said that bein' postmistress was more than she could handle." Edgar was being thoughtful.

Emily was still in her own thoughts, "How about the Grange? You've had an office for many years, must have stepped on some toes... remember the Barker sisters, they applied for membership while you were chairman of that committee?"

"The committee held to the rule, they aren't real farmers."

"Yes, but you were the one to tell them..."

I'm not good at keepin' track of who was offended, or who tried to get some job. Things have a way of balancin' out, I've always said.

"Now you clear outta the house, you've got things to do outside, and I'll need peace and quiet to think through how to get to the bottom of this one."

My Emily is real good at smellin' out the polecat when somethin' has gone bad, so I went to my workshop to let her follow her own ideas.

It took her most of the week, callin' then goin' to see people in the valley, getting' to every meetin' ahead of time and stayin' to talk afterward, makin' notes and drawin' lines on a chart, just like a battle.

When she was almost sure, she got Josie to go with her out to the Barker sisters' house on the East Road. Them two old maids, well they quit sayin' they was thirty-nine several years ago, been in the valley twenty years or more, inherited the place when it had eighty acres of the finest irrigated pasture anywhere. Sold off most of the land and live in the house, even get a housecleaner every week, so they got no business of their own, come to Church regular, but don't do much else.

Emily told me later that the sisters were real glad to have visitors, served tea and little tiny cookies and just chattered away, not suspectin' the real purpose of the visit.

Turns out, sure 'nuff, them sisters started the story.

You've gotta know that I've done handyman work for people in the valley for many years. Nobody could afford to call a plumber from the city, or an electrician, or someone to install an oil-burnin' heater. So, I've made me a cart with a cabinet I can lock, to bring my tools to the job. I've had it for years, so everybody in the valley recognizes it.

Last month I started a job to remodel the upstairs rooms above the Pickle's General Store, to make an apartment for their daughter and new son-in-law. While school was on, I'd work late at night, leave my cart at the job and get in a little work before school the next mornin'.

Them... Barker sisters, I don't dare call 'em what I'm thinkin', thought I was too drunk to go home three nights, because the lower half of that building is the brick Tavern, the only bar in town... and my cart was outside all night!

I was mad 'nuff to go out there and tear their house to pieces, but knew that would only make things worse. so I prayed, and I thought about it till I was sure of my plan.

I waited till them sisters went to bed at night, then I just parked my cart alongside the road in front of their house and left it all night. I'd get it early in the mornin' on my way to work so they didn't see it. I did that three nights in a row and it did the trick!

CHRISTMAS SPIRIT

Dr. Harry Wilson, Professor of Dentistry in the University of California Medical Center, San Francisco, California, worked his way into traffic in his reliable old Oldsmobile. *Where do these damn fools come from,* he thought. He crept up the hill to the home of his friend, Ms. Donna Fleck, Head Librarian for the Medical Center. He calmed down and realized that it was the same fascination for the city that had held Donna and him here. *Relax and enjoy it,* he told himself.

Harry coaxed his Olds up the steep hill and into the driveway of Donna's Victorian mansion. As he rang the doorbell he wondered, *This is one of five Victorian homes in the City which have the designation "Historic Landmark." What's so special about this one?*

Donna opened the door and greeted Harry, "Merry Christmas, and a very happy '04!"

"You are beautiful and I hope you are ready for a memorable evening." Harry held her hand.

"I'm looking forward to meeting Gloria." She responded.

"Let's be off." Harry moved toward his car. He held the door open for her and they headed for the restaurant.

Donna said, "The lights of San Francisco are always spectacular, but Christmas is a magical time of the year. We can travel to any part of the world. China, India, Italy, Spain and Mexico are only a few blocks away. Each neighborhood celebrates in a different way, but the lights and music create a festive feeling wherever you go."

Harry added, "When choirs visited our Center, I loved it when they wore native costumes and sang numbers from their homeland."

Harry pulled to the curb in front of "Dominic's," his favorite Italian restaurant on Judah and let Donna out. Parking in that neighborhood was virtually impossible. Cars blocked the sidewalks and were jammed around vacant buildings. By the time he abandoned his car in front of someone's driveway and returned, Donna was seated at the table he had reserved.

Harry observed that the Christmas decorations were bright, cheerful and done in good taste. Aromas from the kitchen added to the home-like atmosphere. Every seat in the dining room was occupied, and the bar was crowded with people waiting their turn. Sounds of Christmas parties filled the room.

Dominic greeted Harry, "Good evening, Doctor Wilson. This will be an exciting holiday for you, your daughter coming home for Christmas and you just received faculty tenure." Harry had been there Tuesday evening with some friends to celebrate his survival of the evaluation process, which he felt was worse than fraternity initiation rites.

"I haven't seen Gloria for two years, so it's doubly important. You understand, you have children away from home, don't you?" Harry asked.

"My oldest son Phillip" he spoke as he brought a picture of a man in costume out of his vest pocket, "had a singing part in Falstaff with the New York Opera Company. I also have a daughter studying in Japan." Dominic replied.

"He's handsome." Harry handed the picture back, "You are justifiably proud.

"Dominic, have you met Donna?" Harry looked at her as though he hadn't really seen her before. He saw a few gray streaks creeping out under the edges of her radiantly black hair, which was cut short. The first feature he had noticed when he met her was her expressive eyes. She was the head librarian for the entire U.C. Medical Center and was a great help to him when he first joined the faculty and wanted to continue his research on the facial nerve, which he'd begun while he lived in Stockton.

19

Dominic beamed, "Yes, I've known her many years. We all love her. She helped my son Phillip get a scholarship to the music conservatory. He couldn't have made it without her. Oh yes, I know her." He bent and took her hand to his lips.

"Donna, dear, how wonderful." Harry turned toward her. She glowed from the attention, her cheeks were rosy and her smile radiated love. Harry put his arm around her and kissed her cheek.

Donna looked at Harry. "Stop this talk about me, it's your night to celebrate with Gloria, are you sure she's coming?" Donna straightened her jacket and checked the pin on her lapel, a small holly wreath with frosted letters spelling "Merry Christmas."

"Oh yes, she's shopping with her mother, no doubt, and the two of them go into a world of their own, where there is no time limit. I expect her to be late, so let's have some cappuccino." Harry offered.

"She must have a good relationship with her mother," Harry noticed the worry-line between Donna's eyes when she turned and faced him, "they see each other during the year and she spends time with her now. I can't help wondering how she will feel about me. What do you think?" Donna asked.

"Gloria has matured so much while she's been in college, and she handled our divorce quite well. I'm hoping that when she meets you it will be with an open mind and the two of you can create your own relationship." Harry smiled at her. Donna squeezed Harry's hand.

As they were slowly finishing their drinks, a red Porsche swished into the curbside space in front of the restaurant, and out bounced the liveliest Christmas spirit imaginable.

As the Porsche zoomed into traffic, Harry caught a glimpse of his ex-wife.

The doorman ushered Gloria inside, Dominic greeted her and the head waiter immediately was at her side to help with her wrap. He stepped back so Dominic and Gloria could make a grand entrance into the dining room.

Dominic took Gloria's hand as though he was presenting royalty, "Doctor, you should have told me about this dazzling beauty coming to our modest establishment." He turned to Harry, put her hand in his and bent from the waist, "Your daughter."

At a table nearby, six young medical students were celebrating. All six stood and raised their glasses to Gloria.

She played her part beautifully. She held Dominic's hand, smiled and whispered, "Grazie, Signor." Then she turned and blew a kiss to the six young men.

Harry embraced her warmly. She held him tight and kissed his cheek, "I love you, Daddy," her voice broke with emotion, "it's so good to be with you for Christmas.

Harry thought, *I changed the diapers for this little girl, held her when her dolly broke, consoled her after her first break-up with a boyfriend...and*

"Honey, I want you to meet Donna. I've told you about her in my letters. She kept my soul together after I left Stockton." Suddenly he was aware of the contrast between Donna and Gloria. Donna was in gray and black conservatively styled clothes. Gloria wore a bright red and green perfectly tailored outfit. Her coiffure and make-up was freshly done to compliment her natural skin color. Even the scarf and silver bracelet added brilliance to her total appearance without being conspicuous.

"I'm so glad Daddy found you." Gloria bent over and gave Donna a hug.

Donna smiled proudly at Harry. It hadn't occurred to him that Gloria would take the lead in establishing a friendship.

"Thank you, dear. I know how much it means to your father to have you here. My only child is a son, who rarely writes and seems incapable of expressing his feelings."

Harry told Dominic to arrange whatever he thought they would like. He beamed, spoke to the waiter in Italian, then told Harry he'd bring champagne, "on the house."

"Gloria, honey, you look so sophisticated, so mature. I feel like I need to get to know this new woman. What have you done?"

"Oh, Daddy. You used to say something stupid like how tall I'd grown, or how much I'd changed whenever you'd been away for a week or so. I am me. I'll be twenty one in February." She sat up taller and tried to put on a dignified face, but cracked it with a smile.

"I know, you needn't remind me. What ideas do you have floating around in that beautiful head about your future, after graduation?" Harry asked.

21

"Well, there are so many things to do, so many places I'm dying to see, I can't think about all that right now. Maybe after spring break." Gloria smiled.

"Give me a hint. Like one of the things to do and one of the places..." Harry persisted.

"I know I can work for the art director of the New York Community Theater. I want to travel in Italy and Greece. I want to continue my studies..." Gloria tried to respond.

"You wrote that you had some of your work selected for the senior exhibit. How did that go?" Harry asked.

"Didn't I tell you? I get so excited I can't remember who I wrote about what. Three of my ceramic pieces were accepted, more than any other student, and one collage. Sandy got "Best of Show" for an oil, but I got Best Ceramic and Best Collage. So I felt great!" Gloria beamed.

Donna spoke first, "Two Bests? Who judged?"

"Faculty and one distinguished artist. Of course, he worked in oils." Gloria reflected.

"That's marvelous. You must have real talent." Donna placed her hand over Gloria's.

Harry spoke up, "I assume that's when they encouraged you to apply for a scholarship and a teaching fellowship for next year. Are you considering that option?"

"Daddy, don't push me. I'll get around to deciding. Then I'll go about whatever it is."

After the appetizers, Gloria excused herself to go to the ladies room. The dining room was a long rectangle, three tables wide and eight long. Every table was full. When Gloria rose, the noise level dropped. It seemed to Harry that as she walked the length of the room every head turned to follow her, step by step, and that once she was out of sight, people resumed their conversation in a lower pitch.

When she returned, as she neared the table of six young men, one of them called to her and she said something in return.

As she was seating herself, she said "Daddy, that's Warren Edmonton. You remember I had such a terrible crush on him my freshman year in high school that you didn't know what to do with me. He was a senior, quarterback and captain of the football team. I'd know him anywhere." Her cheeks were flushed and her voice raised several tones.

"Warren? Warren Edmonton? I knew he was from Stockton but I'd forgotten he was there the same time we were." Harry offered.

"Forgotten? How could you? I had a slumber party, some boys crashed and we were all in the pool when you came home. You practically kicked Warren as you chased the boys out." Gloria concluded.

"Was he one of them? If I'd remembered that when he had his oral for admission to graduate school, I'd have cut him to shreds!" Harry added.

"Donna, don't you believe it. He's really an old softie." Gloria leaned over and gave her father a peck on the cheek.

Between the soup and salad courses, Gloria responded to signals from Warren and his friends by going over to their table. She sat and talked for a few minutes, then floated back to her father's table on a cloud of happiness.

"Warren is just like he was. Great personality, full of fun. All the fellows think he's the greatest." Gloria persisted.

"And so do you, I take it. Ever since seventh grade, you've come rushing into the house gushing superlative about the newest boy. How come he's always the greatest?" Harry queried.

"Oh, Daddy." She pretended disgust. Harry knew her well enough, she loved it.

When the busboy started to clear the table after the main course, Gloria had Dominic bring Warren to their table.

Harry greeted him, "Warren, join us for dessert. Do you know Mrs. Fleck, our librarian?" Warren towered over them, more than six feet tall, with broad shoulders, bulging muscles and the biggest smile in the room.

"Mrs. Fleck, I worked for you in the stacks part of my first year. I don't think we actually met." Warren offered.

"That's to your credit. I only see the real problems." Her smile put him at ease.

Dominic brought the dessert cart with fancy pastries. Each selected something, which was served with coffee and spumoni ice cream.

Warren and Gloria held hands and whispered to each other. Gloria giggled and laughed.

While Harry was paying the check, Gloria turned to him with her lost-in-the-world-of-love look. "Daddy, Warren has invited me to join his party. All my things are at Mother's, so he'll take me there, after."

"Oh, honey. I had my apartment cleaned today and the bedroom made up for you. I wanted to talk..." Harry hoped.

"We will. I don't leave till the 26th." Gloria tried to sooth him.

I'll take you to lunch tomorrow." Harry pleaded.

"Sorry, Dad. Mom's having open house, and I promised. I'll call you. I promise." Gloria prepared to leave.

Donna spoke up, "Christmas dinner is at my place. I know your father is counting on you. We'll have a few guests and I've asked them to come by two o'clock." Her tone made it clear that she should be there, and on time. Gloria recognized it.

"Oh, I'm looking forward to it. I'll be there. On time." She and Warren stood, preparing to leave.

"Christmas Spirit", escorted by Warren and surrounded by five young medics formed a procession as they exited and flowed into the holiday crowd.

Harry and Donna ordered espressos. He needed time to think, and someone to talk to. "She is so much like her mother, beautiful and spirited. Like a butterfly, she never knows when she will light." Harry summarized.

"She is twenty years old. Let her act like a young woman while she can. You wouldn't want her to be like us, would you?" Donna sipped her drink.

"Heavens no. I looked in the mirror tonight and realized I'll be forty-five in a few months. That's a long way from twenty, and Warren is too immature for Gloria. He still relives his high school sports." Harry was worried.

"He must have some fine qualities to get this far, and Gloria isn't about to make a commitment to any man at this point. Remember, at least you'll have her for Christmas. I haven't had my son with me for three Christmases, since Albert died." Donna had her own feelings about Christmas.

"And she met you. It was wonderful to see the two women in my life getting together." Harry tried to be cheerful.

"It was so easy." Donna whispered as she put her head on his shoulder.

CHRISTMAS DINNER

Harry rang the door bell and wondered, *How old is this magnificent house? Possibly early 1800's...*

Donna, with a full-length apron covering her dress, stood, looking surprised, Harry was an hour early. "Well, come in. I'm still busy in the kitchen."

"I realize I'm early, but I wanted to see you and hoped I could help." He reached to embrace her, but she turned and stepped inside.

Just inside the entry way, a large clump of mistletoe hung from the ceiling. With one long stride Harry stood beside Donna and whispered, "You're beautiful. Merry Christmas." He turned her toward him and kissed her full on the mouth.

While they were embracing, Donna said, "I wondered how long it would take you to do that." With her left hand she removed the apron with a sweeping motion, raised up and with her arms around his neck kissed him long and passionately. They moved a few steps into the living room and fell together on a sofa. After several minutes of uncontrolled emotions, Donna pushed him away and reminded him, "We have guests coming for dinner. You can set the table."

Harry followed her into the kitchen and stood so close their hips touched. Her face was still flushed from the excitement of the previous moments. She said, "Please, I have to prepare a dinner for our guests."

"The smells indicate you are a real cook." Harry offered.

Donna turned toward him and looked up, "I had a call from Gloria, not only is she coming, but asked if Warren could join us. I assured her that was wonderful, and reminded her of the time."

Harry raised his eyebrows, "Warren? Did it sound as though they spent the night together?"

"I didn't hear any sounds." Donna's voice and attitude implied it was of no interest to her.

"You may put the candles on the table. Set it for four. The Daniels can't come, she has a high temp' and may have the flu."

Harry went into the dinning room, out of earshot from Donna. *Gloria stayed overnight at her mother's, and Warren is coming for dinner...well, she is almost twenty one, guess I can't say any more.* Harry ruminated.

What a beautiful place this is, Christmas tree must be 12 feet tall, with decorations that would make a florist shop proud. Red and green colors everywhere, even red berries.

Harry managed to get the candles and silverware on the table. *I know she will change it, but I tried.* Harry concluded. When he returned to the kitchen, his attempt to get an arm around Donna was brushed off, "Not now. We'll have time enough after dinner. I'm assuming the young couple will want to go their own way." Donna didn't look up from the stove.

A few minutes after 2:00 o'clock, the doorbell rang.

Donna asked Harry, "Would you answer the door, I assume it's your daughter and friend."

Warren spoke first, "I'm sorry we're late, traffic was heavier than I expected." Harry reassured him, "No problem. Donna is finishing the dinner."

Gloria put her arms around Harry's neck, "Merry Christmas, Dad. I'm so glad to be with you today."

"I can't tell you how happy this makes me. Merry Christmas to both of you." Harry reached for Warren's hand.

Donna came to greet her guests, "It's the most wonderful Christmas we've had in years. I'm glad you could come." She kissed Gloria on the cheek and gave Warren a hug.

Donna took Gloria's hand, "Would you help with the final preparations?" Gloria gave Warren a "I can't help it" look, and followed Donna.

When they were in the kitchen, Donna looked at Gloria, "My dear, you are so beautiful and talented, no wonder your father almost bursts with pride. Would you or Warren like espresso or cappuccino after dinner? We are having wine with the meal."

"I'd love cappuccino." Gloria replied.

A few minutes later Dona announced, "It's time to take our seats." Harry was at the head, Gloria and Warren side by side and Donna opposite. Harry asked, "Can we hold hands while we give thanks?"

Harry prayed, "Lord, we thank you for the many blessings you have given us, especially to be together in this beautiful setting. Bless this food." Donna added, "I'm grateful for this day, and these good friends."

Harry remarked, "This is a fabulous feast, Donna, you are a wonderful host. We thank you."

Warren and Gloria added, "and we thank you, for great hospitality."

Gloria was too excited to eat meat or stuffing, just salad and cranberries. Warren took turkey and ham, even had seconds. While Warren was finishing his second piece of pumpkin pie, Harry asked Gloria, "Will you stay at my place tonight?

"Mom's one man show starts at three o'clock. I'll stay there after..." Gloria sounded disappointed, but not as much as Harry was.

"But I hoped to have some time with you" he pleaded.

"I'll call." Gloria seemed sincere.

Donna spoke, "Gloria, it sounds like you'll be leaving soon. Come with me, something I'd like to go over with you." Harry looked quizzically at her, but got no response.

Donna and Gloria went to the bedroom, off the kitchen.

"I want to explain something that may be of importance to you, so I'll give you a brochure and other materials you can look at later."

"You may not have heard about the 'Fleck Foundation' which my grandfather started with investments in California real estate and my father increased by investing in raw land near Long Beach. Oil has been producing great profits ever since. I am the Executive Secretary. We make grants to help people in the Arts to study, and get started on their career. You can apply. I will make a recommendation to the Board. Our grants are for one calendar year. You may travel or study or whatever it will take to advance your career. All costs will be covered, and you may re-apply at the end of a year." Donna concluded.

"Why me? You just met me." Gloria inquired.

"Because I know how proud your father is of you." Donna was quite firm.

"I'll study the materials, and let you know." Gloria responded.

"On a personal note, I have two spare rooms in this big house. I would love to have you make this your home, overnight, spring break or longer. You'd be free to come and go as you please, and there are many artists and art programs in this City." Donna stood and opened her arms so Gloria could share a big hug with her.

After Gloria and Warren left, Donna slumped into the sofa and told Harry, "Those few minutes when we held hands and gave a blessing were more significant than all the rest of the day. That was wonderful, and thank you from all of us."

Harry was standing, removing his coat and tie, "Can I call you honey, or dear?"

"As long as you call me, any title will work." Donna grinned.

"Dearest, I'd like a sip of brandy. What can I get for you?" He leaned over and gave her a kiss on the cheek.

"I only have cooking brandy. I'll take a shot of whisky with a chaser of water." She smiled sweetly.

When Harry returned with the drinks, Donna was curled into the end of the sofa. He joined her then raised his glass, "A toast, to Gloria, Warren and us."

Donna added, "As a family."

Donna thought a moment then offered, "Darling, you are justly proud of Gloria. She is beautiful, talented and I learned today, she is level-headed. Come, sit where I can put my head on your shoulder. I want to feel you are close to me."

Harry embraced her, kept her head in his lap, face up, and they shared a long loving kiss. Donna whispered, "If a little brandy will get you into this mood, I'll keep a stock of Christian Brother's finest at all times."

Harry placed his left hand on her breast. She said, "You start that, I'll have to get into something sexy and comfortable. Can you wait a little while, I'd like to 'talk'." She started to get up, but Harry brought her back.

Harry said, "Sit up then, you are too inviting here."

She moved and was half-erect, "You stay here tonight and we can talk and be together as long as we want."

With a big grin Harry asked, "In these clothes?"

Donna chuckled, "Oh, they'll do."

ONE YEAR LATER

Dr. Harry Wilson knocked on the door of Ms. Donna Fleck's Victorian mansion, and went in. She had instructed him to do so, as she didn't want to run from the kitchen to open the door. Once inside, Donna came toward him with arms opened wide, inviting a hug which became a loving embrace and a long passionate kiss. She pushed him away, "Enough of that for now, I have news..."

"I wondered what's so urgent that I was to be here by seven p.m." Harry queried.

"I received this invitation in the mail." Donna handed a white envelope to Harry.

"Notice, it's engraved on finer paper than I could find in San Francisco."

Harry mumbled as he read, "Duke Lombardo, Florence Italy?"

Donna explained, "It's actually the Family of Duke Lombardo."

"A wedding, and you're invited. Oh my God! Gloria is being married?" Harry was shocked.

"She mentioned in one of her letters she'd met the most handsome man in all of Italy. He's an artist, had his work hung in two museums and three galleries from Florence to Palermo. Yes, he's the Duke mentioned, so his wife will be a Duchess. She wants me to be there. What do you think?"

"I won't be invited. Her mother would see to that. When did this come?" Harry remained standing, and walked in a tight circle.

"Today, at work." Donna slid into the sofa.

Harry had a deep frown, "December 18th. DAMN!, I hope you don't mind my swearing, the alternative is to cry."

Donna quickly replied, "Let those feelings out, don't keep them cooped up on my account."

Harry moved a few steps then turned his back toward her. Sobs shook his body, 'till he pulled a handkerchief out of his back pocket, then completed the circle away from Donna. Sniffling with tears on his cheeks, he turned to face her, "Divorce is HELL! You never stop suffering. Her mother, Sally **must** be thrilled. She loves fancy titles but dentist and professor wasn't good enough for her." Harry concluded.

Harry continued to walk in the large living room, he came and stood in front of Donna, "Remind me, how did all of this happen?"

Donna sat upright, " Gloria wrote the best application for a grant I've read. She planned to travel in Italy and Greece to study the two 14th Century cultures with attention to Art as an indicator of their emphasis; Romans, conquest of the known world, to take slaves and build massive structures. The Greeks admired beauty, and worshiped gods and goddesses."

Harry responded, "My daughter was that analytical?"

Donna replied, "She's only been there five months. She is working and studying with a master in ceramics and colored glass."

Harry sat beside Donna, "I need some brandy. Will you have a drink?"

Donna stood, "If you haven't had dinner, I'll fix us something."

Harry stood beside her, "Sounds good, want a cocktail first?"

She smiled, "Just wine with dinner."

They sat on bar stools, at the woodblock work table in the center of the kitchen enjoying lasagna with Merlot wine. After they finished, Harry led Donna to the sofa in the living room and they fell into a loving embrace.

Donna moved into an upright position, looking very serious, said, "We must decide what we will give the couple as a wedding present. Have you given that any thought?"

"Wedding present? Hell No! I didn't even know Gloria was engaged." Harry moved away from any further conversation about the wedding.

Donna persisted, "Well, now you know. Please give it some thought, because I want to attend the. ceremony and would like to let them know what we will do."

"Darling, I'm not ready for that 'WE' about my daughter's wedding. She made the decision."

Donna paused a moment, re-thinking her approach. "'Can we agree to give a reception for them, here in San Francisco?"

"Now that's something I can help with. Yes, it's a good idea." Harry moved closer to her.

"It could be here in the Mansion, or if that's not possible, there are three hotels nearby that do a good job for that kind of event." Her voice reflected her experience arranging social events.

Harry held her hand, "I'll help any way I can. You are wonderful." They kissed and shifted into a comfortable position on the sofa.

Later, as Harry was getting ready to leave, Donna wanted to present one more thought about the young couple, "Doctor Wilson," only used to get his attention, "Yes. Ms.Fleck." Harry could play that game too.

Donna smiled, "I'll leave a thought with you. Gloria needs an apartment, and a studio for her work. We could give her either or both."

Harry gasped. "G' night, Dear." He was out the door.

Monday morning Harry drove Donna to the San Francisco Airport. An experienced traveler, she had one suitcase checked through to Rome, and small carry-on pieces. He avoided conversation about the impending wedding, and she advisedly didn't mention it.

In the waiting area, before Security checks, they embraced and Harry's body was shaking with emotion.

She said, "'Try to think of your own wedding, wasn't it a happy day for both you and your wife?"

"Yes, I suppose so. I know I realized what a big responsibility it was, so enjoyed the reception a lot more than the ceremony." Harry tried to breathe normally.

Harry then added, "Give Gloria my love and best wishes."

When Donna had to move forward, she said, "Darling, take care and recover from the strain of your Final Oral. I'll be thinking of you. Love you."

"Have a good time." Harry responded.

The remainder of Monday and all of Tuesday, Harry struggled to get emotionally prepared for the moment of truth regarding his life and the future. The Final Oral Exam on his thesis and his work at the U.C. Medical Center would be evaluated by the three faculty members and the Chairman of his Doctoral Committee. Technically, they were to consider his Doctoral Thesis and decide if it, and the

author, qualify for the Ph.D. degree. Stories abound about commit-
tees requiring a re-write of the thesis, or even doing all or parts of
the research over. The power of the committee is absolute. There is
no appeal.

Dr. Theodore Manuosois, chairman of Harry's committee, has
been supportive and helpful throughout the five-year process. He
asked Harry to call him "Ted." His last words were, "Relax. Take a
breath before answering a question, look at me then face the person
and speak slowly and clearly. Nothing to it. You've done a good job."
The event, open to the public and announced for all employees of the
University of California Medical Center was scheduled for 2:00 p.m.
Wednesday in the Library.

That morning Harry cut his cheek while shaving, "Damn. It's
been years since I did that." Fortunately it healed quickly and he was
dressed and at the campus before noon.

Promptly at 2:00 p.m., the Chairman and one faculty member
of the committee came in and sat near Harry. The other two faculty
members arrived and took their seats, facing Harry and the Chairman. Ted remained seated, and announced, "This is the Final Oral
exam for Dr. Harry Wilson. I'll ask him to give a brief summary of
his thesis. It will be open for questions from members of his Doctoral Committee, followed by general discussion. Dr. Wilson, you
may begin."

About twenty people sat in chairs behind the members of the
Committee. Harry recognized the three young students who came
to his office to wish him a Merry Christmas. Other than that, the
audience was just a blur.

Because Ted told him, "Three minutes is better than five, which
is the maximum allowed," Harry had written his speech and timed
it at home. He took three and a half minutes, thanked the committee
for their help and sat down.

The youngest, and least experienced member asked, "Why did
you use Chi square to analyze the data?"

Harry remembered Ted's admonition, he took a deep breath,
looked at his Chairman, then replied, "Because for this small
sample, Dr. Manuosois suggested it, and I agreed." Chuckles came
from some members of the audience.

No other questions came from the Committee. Ted rose, "General discussion is now permitted." Each committee member spoke in glowing terms about the fine quality of the research and the preparation of the thesis.

Ted announced, "Hearing no dissenting voice from the Committee, I will announce Dr. Wilson is now granted Doctor of Philosophy, Medical Degree." He shook Harry's hand and said, "Congratulations, Doctor."

Harry stood and shook hands with Ted and members of the Committee. Ted took Harry by the elbow and said, "Let's get a cup of coffee, and talk." He led the way to the staff lounge and brought two coffees to the small table where Harry was seated. He started talking and adding cream and sugar to his cup as he sat opposite Harry.

"That was a fine job. Your committee praised the work, you couldn't ask for anything more. Be sure and get those signatures today. Personally take the final copy to Donna, our Librarian." He paused as he sat down. After one sip of coffee he resumed talking, "I'll send a fax to Mack, and you see him right away. He's head of Publications for the University. I want your book completed in time for our State Annual Convention, next month."

"As Program Chairman, I'm scheduling you as the main speaker for the second day. Get some visuals made, see my secretary, and she will arrange travel and room reservations. Any questions, see her first."

Harry waited to see if there was more, "All this is new to me. Book? Speaker? Are you sure I'm ready..."

"Harry, you have a bright future right here, if that's what you want. Books and speaking engagements are part of that. Yes, you're ready."

That night Harry studied the image in his mirror *Ready? What about Donna? I wish she had been there today. And what about the future?*

Two days later he met Donna at the San Francisco Airport. When she came from the Customs area Harry embraced her, "You are a sight for a lonesome heart."

Donna's response was "'It's great to see you and to be home.'"

As soon as Donna was seated in Harry's car, she said, "Your daughter is a very talented artist. After a few months with a crafts-man working in colored glass, she produced a beautiful piece which I've asked her to ship to San Francisco. I'll have it appraised. What-ever it is I'll send her a check, I want it for my own collection."

Harry asked, "Is it really that good or are you playing fairy god-mother?"

Donna laughed, "I'll be getting a bargain. When I asked her about a reception in San Francisco, her facelit up like a beacon. She'd love it!"

Donna continued, "I asked her to suggest two dates, and I would take it from there."

Harry asked, "What about her husband? Will he come?"

"She said she would ask him, but doubted he would be interested. Going into Florence is a big trip for him. It is about five miles, there are no roads or developed trails. He carries his paintings, walks barefoot so it is an all day adventure."

Harry seemed to let all that sink in, then "So, is she really mar-ried?"

Donna paused, then offered, "The ceremony was in the Catholic Church, only family members attended. I went to the reception where more than thirty people crowded the single room of the 'Manse.' It must have been the family mansion, at least one hundred years ago."

"The bride and groom were there?'" Harry queried.

"In the room, but hardly a traditional romantic pair." Donna added.

Harry's Oldsmobile made it up the driveway to Fleck's Victorian and Harry took her luggage to the front door.

Donna smiled, they kissed and she pleaded travel fatigue, and went in.

Harry returned to his desk at the Medical Center to find a large bouquet of flowers from Donna, with a card, "Congratulations, to the new Ph.D. Love, Donna."

RECEPTION

You are invited to participate in welcoming the rising star of the San Francisco Art World. Meet Miss Gloria Wilson and view her works consisting of colored glass, ceramics and collage plus paintings from Italy where she has been studying and working.

*At the Fleck Historic Victorian Mansion
38 Genoa St.
Sunday, May 12,'04, 2:00 P.M. to 4:00 PM*

*Mrs. Donna Fleck, Host
Invited person and one guest, please.*

(See reverse side for map and parking)
****

RECEPTION

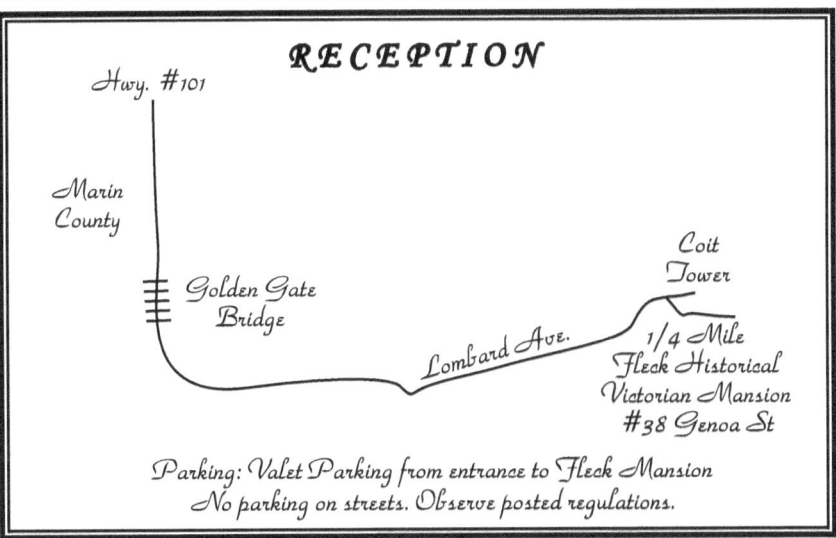

Hwy. #101

Marin County

Coit Tower

Golden Gate Bridge

Lombard Ave.

1/4 Mile Fleck Historical Victorian Mansion #38 Genoa St

*Parking: Valet Parking from entrance to Fleck Mansion
No parking on streets. Observe posted regulations.*

Gloria returned from Italy a month earlier and told Donna through tears, "My marriage was a horrible mistake."

Donna asked,"What happened? You wrote about the most handsome man in all Italy?"

Gloria sobbed, "I must have been blinded by the bright Italian sun. When I painted him in front of the Manse, I saw a gangly, bony frame with a sharp angular jaw, a protruding forehead and sallow complexion. After we met he said all the wonderful things a romantic European could say, including that I was the most beautiful dream he'd ever seen."

"We had two mugs of red wine, called 'Grappo'. It's rough, and powerful. He said he loved me, so we made love before going to bed. He asked me to marry him and I said yes." Tears flowed from Gloria's eyes and she put her face down on the table.

Donna waited a few minutes, then commented, "Honey, please tell your father. He's been upset from the moment we got the announcement."

When Harry arrived he asked Gloria, "How did you get into this mess?"

Gloria looked up at him through reddened eyes, "Edo impressed me as a painter who sold his works regularly and had paintings in three museums. I didn't understand that the title 'Duke' is practically meaningless. He is the third son. The eldest male inherits the title and all property when the current man dies. Reality is they are very poor. The two older brothers won't work in the olive orchards or care for the sheep so there is very little income. Edo keeps what he gets from his paintings, and stays in the dilapidated Manse, which must have been vacant for nearly a hundred years."

Donna asked, "Didn't you love him, the man you married?"

Between sobs, Gloria answered, "I thought so when I said 'yes.' But, by the time the date of the ceremony arrived, I was afraid to say NO, it's a mistake. We slept in separate areas of the Manse. He was already outside and painting by the time I got up. There's no refrigeration, he ate berries and nuts. No water for a shower. One time he brought a pail of slightly muddy water into my space, and said "To wash, and drink. Not much LOVE."

Donna offered, "I can arrange for us to meet with the attorney for the Foundation. He no longer does divorces, but he will recommend a good lawyer."

When Donna and Gloria went to the office, Donna's friend called in a senior partner in their law firm, Mr. Loren Farmosa, specialist in divorce law. He asked Gloria, "Was the marriage consummated?"

Gloria answered, "Not after the ceremony."

Mr. Farmosa stood and with an intent look, asked, "Will you swear to that in court?"

Gloria gave a firm "Yes."

He explained, more to Donna than Gloria, "She could obtain an annulment now, or after six months residence in California, file for divorce."

Gloria asked, "What's the difference?"

"Annulment removes all information about the marriage from the record. A divorce requires publication of the legal action."

"In either case, we must serve the defendant a notice of intent to file an action." the attorney stated.

Donna spoke, "He's in Italy. How do we do that?"

"I'll see that it is done properly." The attorney replied.

Gloria asked Donna, "What do you think?"

"If you are certain that you want out, try for an Annulment." Donna summarized.

Donna excused herself, Gloria stayed to start proceedings to regain her freedom.

Two weeks later Gloria had a call from a deep masculine voice saying, "I'm Jake Plummer, Private Eye. Got a call from yur' attorney, to serve a man in Italy. Well, that's a big country. Where do I start?"

Gloria wanted to be helpful, "Florence is a big city, with a cathedral in the town square. There are three art galleries close by. They know Edo and have some of his paintings for sale. They will direct you to where he works."

"Edo? Is that all the name he's got?" Jake sounded frustrated.

"That is how he signs his paintings. They will know him." Gloria wondered how this man could find anyone.

"You got a picture. Somethin' I can use."

"You don't need anything, just look where they tell you. It's a barren hill, easy to see where you are going." Gloria was so frustrated, she wanted to hang up, but realized this is the man who could help her.

"Sure as hell, don't sound like easy pickn's." Jake ended.

"Have a great trip." Gloria added.

Sunday Morning, Harry was up early, shaved and dressed when he left the guest room he'd occupied and stepped into Donna's bedroom. "Good morning darling," Harry leaned over and kissed her cheek.

Donna slowly moved away, "Whaa, what time is it?"

Harry stepped back, realizing she did not want to be disturbed. Softly he said, "Eight o'clock."

Since there was no response from Donna, he tried again, "I'll make coffee or tea. Hope you get up soon. This will be a great day for you, Gloria and the Foundation." He quietly exited.

Harry thought, *I know better than to try to waken Gloria. She'll get up on her own schedule, breakfast or not.*

Harry managed to make coffee and warm a bagel. He even found some cream cheese that went nicely on the bagel.

Gloria staggered into the kitchen, sleepily made tea and sat opposite Harry. "Why would anyone come to see my work. I'm a kid, just out of college."

Harry smiled, "Donna is so highly respected, when she says you are talented and your work shows it, there will be a crowd."

Tears formed on Gloria's eyes, "My father didn't come to my wedding, 'cause my mother would be there. Now, my mother won't see my first exhibit 'cause my father is here. What kind of family is this?" She slammed her cup on the table and with tears flowing, ran to her room.

Rested and refreshed, Donna came into the kitchen at 11:15 a.m. Harry surrounded her and said, "You're as beautiful as the morning sun. That outfit is cheerful and as bright as the day. You are lovely." She evaded his attempted kiss, "Don't spoil my makeup, there will be time for that later."

Harry held her hand, "Gloria was up earlier, and went to her room in tears. Maybe the excitement, and pressure of the day?"

Donna said "I'd like to see her anyway. Let me try."

Donna knocked on the door of Gloria's room, "Fairy Princess, may I come in?"

Laughter from inside, "Enter, fair Lady," from Gloria.

Harry could hear voices but didn't understand the words as the two women in his life chattered and talked about clothes.

When they came out, Harry marveled at the change in Gloria, "Honey, you are so beautiful that men won't see your art, just how 'smashing' you look today. That outfit is spectacular."

He shifted his attention to Donna, "Darling, standing with Gloria, your dress is just as 'smashing' and your smile is the most beautiful I've seen since I've known you. We are ready for a great day!"

The caterer arrived with food, equipment and helpers.

A representative of security, a company Donna had used before, conferred with her and then quietly went about his business. The students from Cal Med doing the valet parking assembled by the front door and Donna talked with them briefly.

Donna asked Harry, "Stand beside me to greet the guests." The first couple arrived at 1:45 p.m.

When the living room was filled with guests and the wine and pastries were being carried around by the helpers for the caterer, Donna stepped to the center and asked them to clear an area near the sliding glass door so she could introduce the star of this event. When Gloria entered, a hush fell over the crowd, then many women said, almost in unison, "She's beautiful." Men commented to each other, "lot's more than that."

"Friends," Donna began, "for me this is a once-in-a-lifetime occurrence. Our Foundation looks for talented young people, but never have I been so impressed with the recipient of our grant as when I found this beautiful young artist. I've asked her to tell you about her interest in art and the training she's had. Then, samples of her work will be available so you may appreciate the talent she has in several mediums. I'm thrilled to introduce, Miss Gloria Wilson." Generous applause greeted her.

Gloria smiled, "My love of art began when I was a child. High school and a year at University of the Pacific at Stockton stimulated my desire for more intense experiences. Hunter College, New York was a perfect answer."

"When Mrs. Fleck suggested I apply for a grant, I knew a spirit greater than me was caring for me. Italy opened my heart. In that part of the world, art and artists are judged for their true expression of a deeper inner feeling than we seem to have. I tried to reach that level in the works you see displayed here."

Gloria sat down and Donna stood by the colored glass, "You can't fully appreciate the beauty of this piece until you walk around it and see the white cloud move ahead of you."

Donna remained standing as the guests eagerly moved from piece to piece. Several stayed close to the glass, others were drawn to the paintings.

Three owners of galleries hovered around Gloria, "Do you have an agent?" "Will you or Donna negotiate for the sale of these?" "How many more do you have ready for market?"

Gloria smiled and said, "We haven't decided how many to bring to market. Leave your card and we will contact you soon."

Gloria, Donna and Harry sat around the table in the center of the kitchen. Gloria commented, "I couldn't believe, they seemed really interested in each piece. Asked good questions about the meaning of the collage and the landscape in the painting."

Harry offered, "The owners of the galleries were impressed, even asked if I had any of my art for sale."

Donna placed two business cards face down on the table, "We have some good news, the gallery on Mason Street offers twenty thousand for the two paintings. The Getty Museum near Malibu offers thirty thousand for the glass."

Harry picked up the cards, "Is this for real?"

Gloria told Donna, "This is some kind of sick joke, right?"

Donna was serious, "I don't know the man from Getty, but they have money to burn, so I believe it is real. The gallery has been in business longer than I've had the Foundation, I'm sure he is serious."

Harry wondered aloud, "Should Gloria try to get higher bids?"

"It's up to you, honey." As Donna held her hand.

Gloria spoke up, "Donna, the glass is yours. You bought it."

"Honey, you take the Getty offer and pay me back what I sent you, you are the artist, not me."

40

Gloria said, "I don't have the slightest idea about values. I'd be thrilled to take these."

Gloria asked, "I've found a lot in Marin County where I'd like to build my apartment\workshop. Would the two of you, come look at it and tell me what you think?"

Harry looked at Donna then said, "Honey, we'd love to. Even take you to lunch. Tuesday, OK?

Donna changed into something casual so she'd be ready to talk. Harry and Donna curled into the sofa. After a long sensuous kiss, Donna freed herself and faced Harry, "I want to retire in July, so I can devote full time to the Foundation. I don't want to rattle around alone, in this big house. Would you move in with me? We certainly get along very well"

Harry brightened, "I've been trying to say the words, now you've made it easy. Darling, I love you. Will you marry me?"

They both laughed. They continued the caressing and kissing they found so easily.

Two weeks later, the attorney's office called to tell Gloria, "Your annulment was granted this morning. Come in and sign the papers, and you'll be a free woman."

HOMECOMING

Carl left the rental car in the parking lot of a Safeway Market. He walked to Phil and La Donna's house and thought, *"Dad worked for wages on union jobs when we lived in Roseville. How did my brother get enough money to buy this mansion? It's top of the heap, mammoth lot, nothing but the best. La Donna wrote that she didn't appreciate it. No one to talk to, just big-shot businessmen. Phil was the luckiest guy I've ever known, to get La Donna to say yes, and to be set for life with a government contract. What a sucker I was, to join the Marines when I could have stayed here and married La Donna.*

When she opened the door, it brought all the old feelings to the surface. Carl's heart pounded, and his groin came to life, "Hello, Darling," was all his throat could muster.

"What a wonderful surprise!" As she stepped aside for him to enter, Carl saw her in a house dress, but remembered how beautiful she was when they made love in the moonlight after skinny dipping in the ocean, and when they tried to make love in the front seat of his sport car, then gave up and moved to a motel room.

"This was the earliest I could have my discharge." He said.

"Let me get a good look at you," she held the door open.

"I had to wait for transport. I flew with a load of wounded from Saigon to San Diego, then Greyhound to Sacramento. I rented a car with my credit card from before I enlisted. It has my folks' address, so does my driver's license, guess that was lucky. The guy said I looked different, 'till I told him I'd been in Viet Nam."

Carl grabbed her around the waist, "Let's do more than talk." He moved her inside and placed her on the couch, face up, then smothered her with kisses. "I dreamt of you every day, all night and even when I should have been on duty, out there in Nam."

She moved to a better position and whispered, "I've wanted you, every night." La Donna responded to his emotional surge.

He put his right hand inside her skirt above the knee. His left hand fumbled with the neckline of her blouse, reaching for a breast. "Oh darling, wait a second, let me get into something comfortable..."

"While you are doing that, let me get rid of these clothes." Now his voice functioned normally.

They moved to her bedroom, Carl undressed, and she wore the top of a black negligee.

After the excitement of making love, Carl kept his arm under her and held her close. "Nothing in the world could be this wonderful. I'll love you forever."

She softly replied, "Ever since our first loving on the beach at Lake Omega, even though I married Phil, I've wanted you with me, holding me, and protecting me."

At the mention of Phil, Carl tensed and raised up, "What time does he come home?"

"Relax darling. He'd either come by 1:00 right after lunch or not till 7:30 or 8:00. We're safe now." She drew him to her for a long, passionate kiss. But Carl was nervous, "If he thought I'd be here, he'd come through that door long before 7:30, I know him."

She persisted, "Take it easy. All he ever thinks of is work." She raised up to hold his face with both hands and explored the inner ridges of his mouth with her tongue.

But Carl was anxious, "You don't know Phil like I do. He can be mean, real mean. If he finds us in bed, he'll shoot, either of us, or both. No question. "

"He's never been mean to me."

"I know my brother. I don't want to be the one who got you killed.

I've seen 'nuff of that to last a lifetime." He started to get dressed, "Honey, I've got to leave. I don't know where I'll go, but when I can, I'll write to you.

"I Love you. Bye." Carl was out of there.

Carl reached their family cabin overlooking Lake Omega the following afternoon. Phil was outside working on a new shed. "Hi Phil, is that the storage shed we talked about?"

"Aren't you the smart one? It's a storage shed, but not the out-house we talked about. Real concrete and top quality siding and roof." He put down the hammer he'd been using, "So, did you get an honorable discharge?" His body language and tone of voice made Carl feel like he'd been put down again.

"Of course. My Captain recommended, "Special Circumstanc-es." I'd been under fire more than anyone in the Company, and my discharge went right through. Otherwise I had eight months left on my enlistment. I made it to San Diego, last Wednesday, with back pay and a bonus. Not too shabby."

"If you'll quit gabbin' we could finish the shed today."

Carl went in the shed to get some tools. When he looked up at the ceiling, he saw daylight around both of the vent pipes. He found the holder and a tube of silicon paste used to seal openings to make them waterproof. He shouldered a ladder and in seconds he was working on the roof.

Carl wouldn't have heard the ladder go down except his brother Phil yelled up at him, "La Donna is cheating on me. If I ever catch the son-of-a-bitch screwing my wife, I'll kill him with my bare hands."

The minute Carl heard those words, he knew he'd have to take him.

He thought La Donna must have told him, or *the way she denied it, he knew I'd been there."*

Carl carefully worked his way down the roof to the edge, where he was above Phil and only three feet from him. "Big brother," Carl began, "La Donna wasn't a virgin when you married her. Did you expect to reform her while you made all that money?"

"Come down here and I'll show you..." Phil screamed.

Carl moved to the edge of the roof, palms down gripped the overhang for greater leverage, and brought his knees up in front and shoved off. His weight plus the force of his pushing, met Phil's chest full on. Phil was knocked down.

Carl landed beside his brother, and quickly stood and took a defensive stance, to ward off any attack.

Although Phil was dazed, he crawled on hands and knees to retrieve the hammer. He grasped it with both hands, got to his feet and charged Carl, "I'll knock you back to Viet Nam," Phil yelled as he raised the hammer over his head and swung in a wide arc.

Carl didn't move. He ducked inside the intended blow, reached down and grabbed Phil's legs.

Carl jerked hard enough to upset Phil. The force of the intended blow carried him to the left of Carl and Phil ended on the ground.

Carl cautiously circled the inert body, then moved close to feel for a pulse. NOTHING. When he bent down to listen for breathing, he was apprehensive. NOTHING! "OH GOD! HE'S DEAD." Carl knelt beside the body, "Big brother, you made life a living hell for me while I was growing up. But, you're the only one I've got. You gotta live. Come out of it. I need you."

Carl stood up and thought, *I've seen enough death to last the rest of this lifetime. That was war. This is my brother. It looks like he broke his neck when he hit that big rock.*

What should I do now? Call 911? No, that's for emergencies, he's past that.

Call the Sheriff? I can hear him..."You killed your brother? Say it was self-defense, we'll let the jury decide that. Turn around, you have the right to remain silent..."

Fat chance I'd have. It'd be guilty, try to prove I'm innocent. No thanks.

Damn Phil didn't need to get pissed. Nothing would have happened if he'd just left me alone. We'd finished the job. Could've put the stuff in the shed and gone home. But he had to get me one more time, just like when we were kids at the Lake. He had to push me around to show La Donna how powerful he was. Well, he found out I've got some power he never dreamed of.

Carl brought his red Alpha Romeo. which his brother had kept for him while he was in Nam, from it's parking place above the cabin to the shed. He loved it, second to La Donna. Memories flooded in about making love and trips on moonlit nights. He told his beloved partner, "you remained loyal to me, didn't run off with a big shot who'd run you in races, 'nor live with some slob who'd leave you outside."

Carl realized if he left the body outside, animals and birds would tear it apart. He picked up the lifeless form and much like "Nam" threw it over his shoulder and went in the back door of the cabin and thought, "He spent most of his time in the kitchen, so let him rest there."

Carl decided to return to San Diego to retrieve his money and uniforms which were stashed in a locker of the Greyhound Bus Depot. That was good for 30 days.

Two hours later he recovered his valuables from the locker in San Diego, Then he called La Donna's home phone. After listening to her outgoing message "Please leave your number." Carl wanted to check for any incoming messages, like she used to leave for him. His memory clicked in, press star, then enter her code. He remembered… *her birthday? Yeah!* A husky male voice said, "Hi Honey, see you tonight at 8 o'clock. I'll bring the bottle. Be sure and wear that black negligee, the one I like on you".

Carl got a cup of coffee and slouched into a chair. He thought, *"Son-of-a-bitch! She **was** cheating on Phil. Not just with me."*

In less than an hour, Carl and his Alpha crossed the border into Mexico. He told his partner, "The Sheriff can't take me back home from here. We'll just take our time."

TWO MONTHS LATER

Carl stood outside the main entrance to a single storied Mexican style grand home of the owner of a large cattle ranch. He wore a conservative tailored suit of light brown wool. Brown oxfords and a white open collared shirt distinguished him from most cattle ranchers. Two vaqueros stood at his side.

Sheriff Wilkerson arrived from Sierra County, California, in a black Stetson, a silver belt buckle with a raised bucking horse, black ankle-high western boots and a Colt 45 automatic holstered on his left hip. He stood, feet spread apart, seven paces away in bright sunlight. "Carl, I'm here about your brother's death."

Carl greeted him, "Welcome to our Estancia. Always glad to see someone from home. Sorry, my wife is indisposed. We are expecting our first child. I know she will be disappointed to have missed meeting you."

After a pause, since the Sheriff didn't respond, Carl continued. "Get out of the sun. You may come in if you observe our Mexican tradition. NO GUNS in the house."

"No, I'll talk from here. My weapon is part of me." He patted his holster as he spoke.

Carl replied, "As you like. Excuse me, but I have business to take care of." He turned and went inside.

The Sheriff took one step. Both vaqueros moved at the same time. Enrique threw his bolo at the stranger's feet, Roberto was at the side of the Sheriff and successfully twisted his left arm behind his back. They relieved him of his gun.

Carl stood and welcomed him, "Glad you decided to come out of the sun. At this elevation, a sunny day can bring a strong man to his knees. Will you have one of Rosita's margaritas, the coldest and the best in this part of Mexico?"

"No, I will take some cool water." Sheriff Wilkerson seated himself in one of the large chairs near the front door.

Carl remained standing and asked, "You said something about my brother?"

"Yes, I hope you will come home and help us determine the cause of death."

"He's dead?"

"We found him on the floor of his home overlooking Lake Omega."

"When did it happen?"

"His wife, I believe you know her, last saw him October 17, three years ago."

Carl interjected, "Two days after I was discharged, Following two and a half years in Nam. I went to their place hoping to see both of them. Phil wasn't home but I visited with LaDonna. I was disappointed to see what happened to that beautiful and many talented woman. It reminded me of those eggs that some people decorate for Easter. First they suck all the good stuff out, then decorate the hollow shell, worthless things. That's what all that money Phil made has done to her."

"She reported him missing on the 27th of that month. We found the body the next day," the Sheriff added.

Carl continued to walk in circles, near the Sheriff, then further away. "It's no secret, Phil and I were not as close as some brothers." He paused, then resumed "He is all that I had before I came here. What did the autopsy show?"

"His wife didn't want a complete, organ by organ procedure so the doctor said it was a fracture of the vertebrae where the skull and spine are connected. It could have been caused by an accident. Phil had been building a shed on the property. Might have fallen from the roof or a ladder."

Carl responded, "Doesn't sound like Phil. Careful and meticulous, but not reckless."

"What strikes you as a possibility?" This was a kinder, gentler Sheriff.

"Follow the money." Carl was moving slowly around the room, thinking how best to throw him off track. "I don't believe LaDonna is capable of doing it herself, BUT she could get someone else to do it, for money. Did she get that new house and the mountain cabin?"

The Sheriff pondered what seemed to be a new thought, "Yes. As his only surviving heir, and their business."

Carl broke in, "Mighty tempting."

The Sheriff looked at Carl as though wondering if he was an heir.

"No, I'm sure Phil didn't include me in his will." Carl added. Then asked "Who else profits by his death?"

"We've explored those possibilities but come up blank." The sheriff was frustrated.

Carl asked, "Is that some legal document in your shirt pocket?"

"I brought a warrant for you to appear as an interested party, before the Grand Jury of Sierra County."

"You damn fool. You can't extradite me. I'm a Mexican citizen. Talk to the American Consulate, or your District Attorney. Since you have the death penalty, Mexico won't allow an extradition for any offense where there is a remote possibility that the State might execute the person.

"Your presence here is no longer acceptable. My vaqueros will escort you down that slippery trail, and return your gun without ammunition. Mexican police would love to throw a Gringo police officer into a local prison. They don't keep records so it would be difficult for American officials to find you. They could forget you ever existed.

"Hasta La Vista, Senor!" Carl left and signaled the men.

A few minutes later, Carl saw them leading, then carrying the Sheriff to the head of a steep, gravel trail. He faced a two mile journey down a rocky mountainside to the road where he may have left his car.

While watching his departure, Carl suddenly realized, Damn that LaDonna. She set me up. She musta' called Phil to tell him I'd been there. Whatever she said, Phil knew we'd made love in their bed. She told me enough to get me go to the cabin. She knew we couldn't be together without coming to blows.

TWO MONTHS LATER

After the birth of his son, Carl's status greatly improved. Naming of a son, especially the grandson of a man of great distinction, requires time and careful consideration. Carl politely stepped aside.

Before the Christening, Senor Bustamente came to Rosita's bedside, where she was caring for the baby. With Carl holding her hand, he told her, "I'm meeting my legal advisors this evening to arrange the transfer of the title and all property connected with the cattle operation to you and your wonderful husband, Carl. I am so proud of you and know you will protect the family name."

The three of them drank toasts to the future and good health for the baby. Tears of joy streamed down Rosita's cheeks.

Carl realized this was a great opportunity for him and his family. One of his first official acts was to designate his closest friend and buddy from 'Nam, Enrique Menqez as Foreman, in charge of the animals. Carl told him, "You saved my life and members of our squad many times. This is only a partial repayment of that debt. I know you are the best man for the job." They fell into an embrace, tears fell from the heart of each man.

A Greek philosopher said, "The Alpha to Omega, is a complete circle." OR what goes around comes around.

OH YE OF LITTLE FAITH

JoAnn Sorenson, with more gray than brown hair cut close around her pudgy face, paused to adjust her long skirt, gave the appearance of the preacher's wife coming to call. She knocked on the door of a narrow, old trailer smothered with vines where her new patient lived.

"Come in" came from a husky, masculine voice.

Smells of urine, cigar smoke and rotting food assaulted her, as she walked the few steps needed to approach the figure in a wheel chair, huddled next to an unmade bed. "I'm JoAnn. A Hospice volunteer, here to do whatever I can to help."

"Didn't ask for noth'n, 'less you can help me die."

She stood at his feet. All she could see was the hood of a black, tattered sweatshirt and his beak-like nose that protruded through uncut facial hair. His dark brown eyes were lined with veins and between the forefinger and thumb of the left hand he held the remains of a cigar with an ash dangling from the unlit end.

"What is your full name? My sheet merely says Renaldo." JoAnn asked.

With the faintest hint of a smile, he answered. "Renaldo da Vinci. From a long line, going back to Leonardo, the great artist, engineer and astronomer."

"My, that is impressive. Have you been to Italy?" JoAnn asked.

"When I was 17 the family sent money for me to come home. I'd left when I was 6, so didn't remember much about the place. I was very excited and made the trip. Soon, I realized they expected me to stay, care for my aged grandfather and the family farm. There were a few scraggly olive trees and some sheep almost as old. The climate in Sicily is balmy and warm every day. Damned if I didn't hate it, the same all the time. No changes for the seasons!" He grimaced and tried to shift his weight in the chair.

"Compared with Minnesota where I grew up, that would be ideal. Forty below zero by Christmas was regular, and one hundred degrees during harvest was expected. Yeah, the seasons changed, but rarely for the better." JoAnn cleared dirty dishes and litter from the kitchen table.

Renaldo stirred and said, "I fell in love with the warmest brown eyes I'd ever seen. Gina was a beautiful girl. Her touch aroused every fiber of my being, her kiss carried me to heights I'd never experienced. She was warm, loving and caring."

"She wouldn't come to California with me so I was tempted to stay. My Grandfather died, and the Mayor told me I now owned the family farm. After the funeral, I came home to Santa Maria, California ." He seemed lost in his memories.

"Are you a doctor?" Renaldo moved toward her.

"No. I've worked as a nurse, changed bedpans and cared for patients in nursing homes 'till I found a place to live that I can afford. I volunteer when I want to."

"Think of it this way, you got to see your family and fell in love. Many of us don't get to do either." She paused and since he didn't speak, offered "You get lunches from Meals on Wheels, so I'll fix supper next time I come. I'll be here twice a week, if that's okay with you."

She saw a movement of his mouth but didn't hear anything.

"Nice meeting you, Renaldo. See you next Tuesday." JoAnn left quietly.

As she walked to her car, she went around his house admiring the wisteria and bougainvillea that had been woven into trellises and allowed to completely cover the side of the building. From a distance, "It provides an oasis in the arid, dusty land that was barren on all sides," she thought.

JoAnn brought fixen's for a pasta supper and a large saucepan with the tomatoes and other necessities because she hadn't seen any utensils in the cupboard.

"Renaldo, I want you to work up a good appetite, for this will be a treat, guaranteed." She placed the food on the kitchen counter.

"You're a busy little beaver. I never said I wanted…"

She cut him off, "Let's make a deal, I'll fix the supper and you try each dish. If you don't like it, I'm out of here. Agreed?"

"You don't leave much choice, Okay." He returned to the side of his bed.

She started making the sauce and preparing the pasta, waiting for him to speak. Then she realized he lit a new cigar, and when she moved to see what he was doing, he was pouring a goblet of red wine. "I'll set the tray of appetizers on your night stand so you can get started."

"I'm fine," was his abrupt reply.

When the sauce was at a point where it would simmer awhile, she pulled a chair in place to talk with him. "Tell me about the farm in Italy."

Without looking at her, Renaldo slowly released a cloud of smoke. "It's in Sicily, people there don't feel like they belong to the mainland. Grandfather's place ain't much compared to California farms. It's a few hectares on a steep rocky hillside. Old stone house which is nice and cool, with sheds for sheep and storing olives."

"Grandfather claimed Leonardo was his great grandfather. Well, that's just not possible. He couldn't draw worth a damn, nor cut a straight edge with a saw. He sure as hell weren't no farmer. No place for a young man." He slid back in his chair like that much talking was a great effort.

Renaldo, still looking off into space, added, "Guess each of us has some good times and lots more bad ones. I had 'dirt' jobs before I got on in the Nursery, over near Vandenburg. The owner assigned me to the big greenhouse for exotic plants. Made me an offer I couldn't refuse; my own boss, monthly salary, 'Just don't lose any of those plants was the way he put it."

They dined on pasta with warmed French bread with garlic spread inside the two halves. Renaldo's wine was what he called Dago Red, then explained. "I worked for an Italian farmer who had produced a red wine through the prohibition years. He sat a barrel outside his barn, self-serve (bring your own bottle, leave some

52

money in the coffee can) which everyone called Dago Red. He now markets that wine as Chianti-Bravo, for more per bottle than he used to get for a gallon jug."

When Renaldo finished his second helping of pasta they were quietly enjoying the pleasure of good food, and a pleasant evening. JoAnn sipped slowly and he poured another glass for himself. "That was the best pasta I've ever had in the U.S.A. Tried it in New York, Chicago and San Francisco nothing comes close. You are a wonderful cook, and a great caregiver."

"Thank you, Renaldo. My Mother was a good teacher. It's all in the tomatoes, right variety and just early ripeness."

After a long, silent pause, Renaldo looked into space and asked, "Do you believe in Heaven?"

Since that was the first time he'd raised a question about life or death, JoAnn was somewhat taken aback. "I'd answer yes, then like to explain."

"Go right ahead" he answered as he swung his wine glass toward the ceiling.

"I've believed in God and Jesus Christ most of my life. Prayed for forgiveness, and given thanks for many blessings. My body is wearing out, but the Eternal Spirit within will live forever. Maybe this is Heaven, right here. If not, it will be something better."

"See, I expected something like that. Hell, there ain't nothin' after this is done. Can't prove all that stuff 'bout God." He put his wine glass on the table, fired up a new stogy and moved back close to the bed.

She cleaned up and left, "See you in two weeks, Renaldo."

JoAnn came to see Renaldo three weeks later, "Renaldo, I want you to know that I didn't have anything to do with you being off the eligibility list for Hospice. My supervisor told me she had visited, and you had improved so much that others on her list were more deserving."

"Yeah, she was impressed. Said you were one of the best she'd ever had. Now, I need you more than before. I'll double your pay if you'll come." He slid back in his chair.

She laughed, "Two times nothing is still nothing. I'm a volunteer." She moved beside him, and smiled.

"How 'bout twice what people who do that work get?" His voice carried his message, he wanted her to come.

"That's real generous. Let's settle on $15 per hour. Two hours a visit and I'll be here twice a week." She half turned away, never having had to strike a bargain that way.

"Sounds good to me." He took out a cigar and started to fire up.

She headed for the door, "See you Tuesday, Boss."

SIX MONTHS LATER

"Ed, besides this da Vinci matter, how many cases have you got for the rest the month?" Eldon, representing the State of California asked.

"You know damn well, only two small ones." Ed responded.

"For Christ's sake, why do we have to be in the basement of the County Courthouse, no windows and two years of dust on every table?"

"Eldon, you'd bitch about your own funeral. I can't use a court-room, the County won't let me and the State won't pay rent for a decent place. You know I'm just a Referee, not a judge."

"I know that, but you could raise a stink in the Legislature..." Eldon caught himself, remembered Ed was an Independent who once was on the Republican Central Committee. He wouldn't be welcome in Sacramento.

They found an immense room, musty from the lack of ventilation, with dust covering tables and chairs. The two men turned one library-sized table across the far end of the room, which formed a two-sided space with rows of tables and chairs for participants and visitors to see the Referee.

Ed pulled a chair to the middle of the large table and spread documents across the surface.

Eldon sat closest to his left side. From experience he found Ed's hearing wasn't good on the other side.

Ed mumbled, searching for the agenda that he'd prepared only an hour earlier. "Here's the damn thing." Hearing's scheduled for 11:00 a.m., so we'll wait another ten minutes. The only litigant who re-quested an audience is for the trailer park on the deceased's land."

Eldon spoke up,"How about the Italian property?"

"I sent a notice to the mayor of the town, never heard a word. Should be 'nuff, 'less you or somebody else complains." Ed was still puffing from moving that table and some chairs.

"You know I'll never complain." Eldon grinned.

A business suit from Men's Warehouse, on a slender blond young man, with large wire rimmed glasses meekly entered the room. "Is this the hearing for the disposition of property left by Renaldo da Vinci?"

Ed turned to face the questioner, "Just what caused you to ask such a question?"

"I'm representing Mr. Zumbrowski, owner of the trailer park..."

"Oh God!" Ed exclaimed. "Did you pass the latest bar exam?" His disapproval of the intruder was obvious.

JoAnn Sorenson entered and walked in a stately manner the length of the room and approached the side opposite the seated attorneys. Referee Ed Wilson stood, and in an effort to be formal, said, "I'm glad to have such a distinguished, lovely lady grace our lowly hearing room."

JoAnn replied in a low, modulated voice, "I'm honoring your request."

Just as Ed was regaining his composure, a young woman entered and, while her eyes adjusted to the light, stood still.

Ed and the other men turned to watch every movement of her lithe body. A small circular, black hat sat precariously tilted on one side, perhaps to allow the swath of deep black hair to move freely with every burst of energy released by the lady. The bright spring colors of her form fitting dress, and the light in her eyes awakened the little audience.

Ed cleared his throat, and tried to speak but it was a stammering, "LLL, OOOO" that came out. Eldon rose, "Come in, whoever you are, and we hope you are in the right place."

She was more than half way to the big table and spoke, in a soft, high pitched voice, "I'm Carmella, from Sicily." She took the chair closest to JoAnn.

Ed regained some composure, "Miss da Vinci, I welcome you, and hope your stay in our fair city will be to your liking." He sat down and fumbled with some papers.

"I'll summarize the assets of Renaldo da Vinci, then allow time for questions.

"In savings and CDs, there is $200,000. An Ordinary Life policy with Metropolitan Life Insurance, face value $200,000, with an accrued value of $285,495. The real estate in San Luis Obispo County, zoned agriculture/light commercial...I haven't had an official appraisal but the real estate broker for that area said, "As undeveloped agriculture acreage, $5,000 an acre is an average price." If, in fact, there are 15 acres, about $75,000 is what I'll use.

Ed looked at Carmella, "Miss da Vinci, do you wish to present a claim?"

She rose, checked her hat which was still in place, then smoothed the tight fitting dress with slender hands and movements more like a ballet dancer than a young woman addressing a dignitary of a strange country. Her smile caused Ed to lean backwards, almost losing his balance.

"Your Supreme Justice, I beg your indulgence, my English is insufficient to express my joy to find that you are considering my humble request. My friend, the Mayor of our modest village, San Loretto, sends his wishes that you will find it possible to..."

Ed interrupted, "Please, state your request. Then provide any supporting evidence."

Both attorneys reacted and told Ed, "Let the lady continue."

Ed nodded and Carmella stood, checked her hat then with a sweeping gesture, her left hand went around her left thigh and across her midsection to get the skirt into the right places. Her hand shook as she brought the papers into position, "Your Honorable Referee, I wish to present my birth certificate showing Renaldo da Vinci as my father and the gold certificate from my friend the Mayor describing the farm which my father owns. I beg you to consider these valuable credentials as proof for who I am." She smiled demurely, placed the papers where Ed could get them, then reversed the process of getting her dress ready for being seated.

Ed thanked her, and announced, "I'll move now to the distribution of the estate. No claims have been submitted for outstanding debts. California law provides for the State to take all assets when there is no will or other legal document stating how the deceased wished to have them distributed. As Referee I'm charged with the responsibility of hearing all claimants, considering the merits of their position and developing a plan, which we will now do.

"First, Ms. Sorenson, the Coroner found a note wanting you to be rewarded for your devotion and friendship. Since there were no witnesses, or verification by a notary public for his signature, I can not consider this a legal document."

"I believe that was his wish so I am assigning the trailer house where he lived, with one acre surrounding the house to Ms. Sorenson. In addition an award of $20,000 to provide for the upgrading needed to meet the building code. Details to be worked out with the County."

"For our guest from Europe, I am pleased that she provided a birth certificate and letter from the Mayor. The title of the family farm will be transferred to her. To cover her expenses, travel and getting the farm in her name an award of $10,000. To bring the farm up to current standards, with a chance of making a living, I'm awarding $40,000."

"Miss da Vinci, if you have questions, please call my office. This could be done before the end of the week if there are no objections." Ed looked directly at Eldon for emphasis.

Carmella rose, "Thank you your Majesty."

Ed was on a roll, gaining confidence with every award.

He faced the two attorneys, "We have a real can of worms with this real estate. The underlying title shows that the deceased filed a homestead, proved up on it and recorded it in his name. There is no record of a sale or a lease for the trailer park. I didn't talk with Mr. Zumbrowski but the occupants of the trailer park told me they paid a modest rent, and seemed happy. Four men had in their possession a "Bill of Sale" for the purchase of the space which each occupies.

"San Luis Obispo County will have a claim for failure to obtain approval for the park, no business license and property taxes for the years since occupancy."

"We can't deal with all this today. It is lunch time so I suggest you two men get acquainted and return by 1:30. Let's see where we can go next."

Ed addressed the ladies, "I'd love to take you to lunch, but the judge who supervises this proceeding will meet with me to see my report. You are welcome to be here this afternoon, but all of the business will be between the attorneys and me."

Everyone stood, JoAnn greeted Carmella and they walked arm in arm toward the exit. "Would you like to see where your father lived?" JoAnn played the role of a stepmother.

OUR BIG BREAK

"Hi, I'm Patti Nielson," she said as she handed a business card to me, Chuck Walters. We were in the I.O.O.F. Hall in Montebello, California, where two buddies and I were playing a 'freebie' for the Jobs Daughters. I'm playing alto sax, Eddie is trombone and Mitch plays piano or string bass. We are three college students who enjoy playing swing band numbers.

She continued, "My little sister told me, 'Ya gotta hear these guys, they are the greatest...'" I'm planning the annual ball for the Junior Woman's Club of Pasadena and need a band that will get the crowd dancing."

I interrupted, "We're not a band, what you see is what you get. Sorry lady, I gotta get back with my friends. There's a soda fountain downstairs where I'm a part-time 'soda jerk.' Meet me later, I'll finish here in thirty minutes."

Her smile would charm the testicles off a bronze statue. "See you downstairs." She winked.

I told Mitch and Eddie, "If you'd like to meet her, join us at the soda fountain."

Mitch offered, "She's from Pasadena, looking for a band. We're a trio at best, no thanks. You take care of her."

Eddie was putting his trombone in a case, "Gringo, No thanks. You can have my part of that one. I gotta go home to my sweetie."

While I waited for her, I reviewed my first impressions. She's short, attractive and well groomed. In Pasadena, women dress up for every trip downtown. This one is professional, an executive, doctor or something where she makes real money. Then I remembered her business card, "Associate Loan Officer, PASADENA SAVINGS & LOAN. That's only a block from Pasadena City College, where the three of us go to school," I thought.

I held the side door open for her. She had changed into a blouse of soft material that caught some light to accentuate the femininity of the lady and beige slacks, which proved she may have played on an athletic team.

Because it was after hours for the pharmacy, I turned on the light in the back room. "I can fix a fountain drink, what would you like?"

"Coke, no ice, will be fine." Her perfume sang of spring flowers.

We took our cokes to the counter where the pharmacists fill prescriptions. She sat on a stool and looked directly into my eyes, which was disconcerting to say the least. I sat close to her on another stool.

"What does Chuck want to do in life?" she asked.

"Right now I'd like to feel comfortable, without personal questions, please. That's a nice wedding ring you are wearing." My palms were sweaty.

She leaned close to me and in a low, sexy voice said, "Chuck, the two of us can work this out so you have fun playing the tunes you love and the Junior Women will have a great time."

I stammered, "Sounds good to me, if I can sell my buddies on the idea."

Patti placed her hand on my left knee (every hormone in my body broke into flames).

She said, "The way they followed you tonight, you could sell them a trip to the Sahara Desert. I need a five piece band, with a vocalist..." Patti was determined.

"I could try to find two guys..." I mumbled.

She smiled, watching my face, "You realize that a vocalist would complete the venue, don't you?"

"Sure, and Santa Claus will come at Easter. I don't know anyone to contact in Pasadena. I could post a notice, then take two or three weeks to interview and try them out. Lady, I'm a full-time student, music is just for fun."

"There are seven weeks to prepare…" She persisted.

Patti spent some time with her Coke before continuing, "Student, soda jerk and musician, you must like to get paid while having fun. Let's try again. I need a band. I liked what I heard tonight. Would you try to get two more players and make an effort to find a vocalist?"

"You haven't said how much money. If I'm to do that and schedule rehearsals, I need to be rewarded." I slid off the stool and stood a full step away from her.

Patti raised her eyebrows and smiled. "Sorry if I've made you uncomfortable." I didn't react. "I've budgeted $25 per musician."

I replied, "That's a good starting point. How about a sound system and an operator?"

"That's part of the rental agreement for the hall." Now she was relaxed.

"Stage lights and a spot?"

"Done." in a tone to end the conversation.

"I'll see if my buddies are interested, then get back to you."

"You know, Chuck, you are tall, handsome and talented. You'll be successful wherever you go…" She stood so close to me her body touched mine. My heart skipped a beat.

She continued, "You would have a great career in the real estate loan business. I'd like to introduce you to our president and take you to lunch."

"Thanks for the offer. I'll call you, either way. You will have a great event." I concluded.

TEN DAYS LATER

I called a few minutes before 5:00 p.m. and got right through to Patti. "First, let me apologize for my attitude that evening. I was very insecure in the presence of a beautiful professional lady."

"Thanks for the compliment, you were just being business-like." Patti was cheerful.

"I have some good news. A piano player who has worked with us agreed to join us and has already been in two rehearsals. He'll be okay and Mitch can play string bass, his favorite."

"That's great. And a drummer?" she asked.

"We'll find one, here at PCC. Plenty of interest there." I just stated what we knew.

"So, the big question, have you had any luck locating a vocalist?" Patti wondered.

"Glad you asked it that way. The piano player told me about a girl who stopped the Spring Music Festival last year. The only one to be called back for an encore, then a second chorus of her last song.

"I met her on campus. She's a knockout for beauty and personality. Here's the catch. Her father controls every movement of that girl. He despises musicians. I talked with her mother, who seemed very nice, but I'd have to talk to her father.

"It's time for you to use your best persuasive voice. Get an appointment with father, and convince him we won't have time to rape her."

"You want ME to do your recruiting?" an incredulous Patti responded.

"I can't get inside their house, do your best for the Junior Woman's Club of Pasadena."

"Put that way, I can't say no. Give me their name and phone number."

THE FOLLOWING WEEK

Patti left a message for me to call her. "I've good news!" before any greeting. "Mary Lu will sing with your group. Her father will bring her and take her home. You can arrange rehearsals with her." She was all business.

"Patti, I knew you were good, but that goes way beyond any expectations. Thanks, it'll be a great show, for certain."

I added, "We rehearse every Wednesday at 4:30, drop by the Orchestra Room."

"Great idea. See you then." She hung up.

PASADENA JUNIOR WOMENS CLUB
ANNUAL BANQUET AND DINNER DANCE
PASADENA WOMENS CLUHOUSE
OCTOBER 16, 1938   7:00pm-12:30am
$20.00 per couple

By 8:00 the five of us were on the bandstand, so I gave the beat and we were off. "A String of Pearls" was a safe bet. We were in tune and together. A few couples came to the floor.

Mitch signaled 'slower,' so I nodded to Eddie and the piano player. For the second chorus we were as slow as we could get and the floor was crowded. I was amazed when we finished, they gave us a generous round of applause. WOW! They liked us!

"Start Dust" brought a few more couples onto the floor. They were dancing as though they really enjoyed it. Patti and her partner came near the bandstand and gave us a big smile.

What a relief.

After several sets of big band music, I picked up my clarinet and moved to the mike. Ladies and gentlemen, we are going to the birthplace of modern jazz, Nworleens. When a black musician dies, a traditional ceremony starts in Basin Street. Mitch moved to the piano, I am on my clarinet, in the "basement," low, slow and sad. "Basin Street is the street"... A few mourners form a single line, women in bright colored skirts, each with a small umbrella twirling overhead, they strut their stuff. The group grows in number as they approach the meetin' house where the funeral service will be held.

I'm now into the chorus "...where the white 'n dark folks meet." mid-range and normal tone.

After the service, a celebration begins. Dancin' in the street, anyone can join in. "When the Saints Go Marchin' In." Now I'm climbing stairs to the clouds... "I want to be in that number."

For the first time I look at our dancers, nearly every guest is on the dance floor, "...when the saints...go...marchin'...IN!" Now I'm in clouds on a sweet riff.

Great applause and cries of 'encore' greeted us for the first time, what a wonderful experience.

Twenty minutes before intermission, May Lu and her father came in the side door. I motioned for her to come on stage.

"Ladies and gentlemen, we are about to have the treat of the evening, A lovely young lady, a student at Pasadena City College, stopped the Spring Music Festival last year. The applause for her first number required an encore and a repeat of the chorus of that number. The 'Star News' was high in their praise of her talent and that performance. We are honored to be on the platform with her. Our own 'Mitch' will be her accompanist.

"Introducing Mary Lu Shapiro, singing an aria from the opera La Boheme." Polite applause greeted her.

Mitch gave several bars of intro. With her opening phrase a hush came over the audience who gathered in front of the bandstand. As she finished, there came an outpouring of enthusiastic applause and cries of "More," "Encore."

She bowed and moved close to the piano, "Now stomp your boots, clap your hands and holler...theme from the musical, Oklahoma." The crowd loved her, gradually at first, then swelled to a crescendo of yells and applause. It was genuine emotion – love and fun!

She was gracious and laughed with joy. As she left the stage I told them, "Don't stray too far. Fifteen minutes for intermission, then Mary Lu will return to open the second half of our show."

Eddie and I took Cokes to a secluded table in the rear of the dance floor. "Well, Gringo, you did one hell of a job. They love you." Eddie outdid himself, he rarely gave anything more than an okay.

A man with a fringe of white hair, a beer-belly to go with what had been a tailored suit ten years ago, faced me and threw a business card face-up in front of me. He pulled a chair from a stack and sat facing me.

In an accent that came from Iowa many years earlier, he said, "I'm the owner and manager of the Big Bear Lake Resort 'n I want dance music, not the new 'hog-callin' stuff Hollywood is sellin'. This crowd sure likes what yur peddlin'. I'd like you to come to my place for a weekend, play Friday and Saturday and if you like it and my crowd likes you, I'll offer you a summer job."

By his mannerisms and voice, he expected Eddie and me to jump at the chance. "Mister," I looked at his card but couldn't read his name, "Big Bear Lake. First of all we are trying to relax...as for a summer job, I have one lined up and Eddie is recently married and started his own business. Don't think any of us would be available. We are students first, playing music is for fun. Thanks, but no thanks, and we have to get back to work. I'll keep your card and call you if we are interested after we finish this job."

We started to return to the stage. I walked ahead and Eddie looked for a restroom. I heard Mitch, doing what he called "warming up." His fingers float over the keys, occasionally touching enough to create a sound. Then, two chords which I recognized... what the... is he starting without us?

Mary Lu crouched into half-size, imitating a train engine starting, arms like pistons moving. It was the introduction to "Chattanooga Choo Choo."

With this number she stole the whole banana. Every person in that room, including employees, stopped and gave her full attention. I went to the rear of the platform without my instrument. Eddie was on the far side, without his horn. Her body moved in perfect harmony with the music. "There'll be a certain party at the station..." was so real we knew her lover was a great musician.

The cheers and applause overwhelmed her. She enjoyed being on stage, and we loved her.

She came center stage, "Thank you, thank you. I'll conclude with my favorite dance number and I believe it's one of Chuck's. "Little Brown Jug."

Mitch's left hand rumbled and she stayed front and center to sing and move separate parts of her body. I improvised on my alto sax, Eddie supported the bass and it was a great swing number.

At the start of the second chorus, I put my sax in the stand, faced her and spread my arms. She touched my outstretched arms, then I turned her out left, back face to face, then to the right. She signaled with her eyebrows "up," I nodded and when she turned in, as light as a feather, she came straight up and put her face over my left shoulder to give an impish smile, then quickly down and duplicated the move, face over my right shoulder with a smile that caused the audience to crack up.

Back down, out wide to the left, face in, now into the center with a swoop... left leg touching the floor, her hair was flowing onto the stage with my left hand barely supporting her.

Up and bow to the crowd.

Cheers, applause and many favorable remarks. A completely fantastic performance!

She disappeared out the side door.

"This number is ladies choice," I announced to get the crowd back into their own party.

Two numbers later, I announced, "Next number will be the last dance." Oh, no! came from many of the guests. "We will conclude with "Moonlight Serenade." To the technician, "Lights down low."

The only thing left was "Good Night Ladies" with most of the men signing to their partner.

"Thank you for inviting us, it's been a great evening!" Lights up and time to pack and leave.

Five of us met in the coffee shop near PCC campus. "I have some tip money to divide." Mitch said, "The girl stole the show. We were at our best for her."

Eddie added, "Like I said, your bit about Neeeorlens was d' best I've heard you do."

"How 'bout our drummer?" "Didn't know what to expect, lots better 'n any rehearsal. Yeah, I'd work with ya again."

"Remember," I said, "write the name of a song on a five dollar bill... well we have four bills. Patti's partner gave us seven dollars for 'gas money.'"

I'd suggest we give Mitch and Eddie their gas money, then divide the rest four ways. I won't take any, my $25 from Patti is enough.

"Hey Guys, the owner of the Big Bear Lake resort cornered Eddie and me during intermission and wants us to try out for a summer job at his place. Work a weekend, Friday and Saturday nights for dancing. Anyone interested?"

Mitch offered, "Tell him $25 per man, per night. Plus room and board, only if he can get Mary Lu."

"Yeah, o.k. came from the others."

In a few minutes it was done, with handshakes we each headed home.

Needless to say, I never heard from the Big Bear Lake guy.

PASADENA SAVINGS & LOAN

A week after the Banquet, Patti called. "My boss, the President of this company, wants to take us to lunch. Can you be here by 11:00 O'clock Friday?"

"Lunch? What's this about?" I asked.

"Bruce'd like to meet you. He's heard enough from me, but a couple of the husbands who were at the banquet gave him their impressions and that made it official." Patti laughed.

"I'm always glad to have a free lunch, and joining you makes it special. Sure, I'll look forward to it. What should I wear?" I wasn't sure why I'm invited.

" Whatever is natural." She concluded.

When I arrived at an inconspicuous office building, Patti met me at the door. She opened her arms to greet me, pulled me close and said, "Don't be surprised by anything that happens today." She kissed my cheek, and led me into the executive suite. It was larger and more elegant than any I'd seen in the movies.

"Bruce" was more than six feet tall, with light brown hair carefully groomed. He wore a beige, silk, open collared sport shirt which exposed some of his Palm Beach tan. He came around the corner of the massive desk with his manicured right hand extended, "Chuck, I've heard more compliments about you than any C.E.O. in Pasadena. There must be magic in your touch. Thanks for coming. I just had to see for myself . Have a seat and let's get acquainted."

"Thanks. Do I call you Bruce?" I couldn't believe what I just heard.

"That's my name. Of course." He smiled and stretched his long legs under the desk.

I fumbled for a minute, *what can I ask?* "I'll confess, I don't know a thing about a savings and loan. How does it work?" A feeble effort.

After half an hour of his questions and my answers, he got to the point. "You have the intelligence and personality to be very successful in this business. I want you to work with us this summer, as a management trainee. I'll show you the ropes and even give you your own clients when you are ready."

"I already have a job. In the accounting office of the City of Montebello."

He didn't blink, just went right ahead, "I'll double whatever you'd make there, and add something I'm sure they can't match. I'll pay your tuition at any college you want to attend." He smiled with the satisfaction only seen at a poker table when a player has a pat hand.

I mumbled, "That's mighty generous. I'll certainly consider it."

He rose out ot the chair to stare into my eyes, "CONSIDER? What else is there to say?" He slid back to his original slouch.

Silence was heavy. He reached for the phone, "Patti? Are you ready?"

She must have said yes, for he rose and motioned to me, "Let's go. Doesn't pay to keep a lady waiting."

The driver of a long black limousine was holding the front door open for Bruce. Patti and I sat in the soft leather cushioned rear compartment. Not a word was spoken about our question and answer session. She cuddled close and dropped her hand along the inside of my right thigh. Less than ten minutes later we were ushered into the dining room on top of the tallest building in Pasadena. It was equal to the best of London or Paris.

The food was excellent, and the service matched the elegance of the decor. Bruce signed the bill and we were escorted to the car. There was small talk, no mention of business.

As Patti and I got out, Bruce turned to me and said, "I'll hear from you." More a command than a farewell. He was gone.

We climbed into Patti's Jaguar and zoomed to her up-scale home overlooking the Rose Bowl and the Sierra foothills. Spectacular views, and fantastic landscaping spoke of money to spare.

We entered her living room to see modern art and decor. She lifted her face for a long, sensuous kiss. Patti said, "I'll only be a minute. Make yourself a drink, or whatever..."

I relaxed in a big, comfortable lounge chair and wondered *what does all this mean? Savings and Loan, what am I doing here?*

I rose to meet her when she returned in a chinese style silk jacket which revealed more than it concealed, and long black pants of a similar material, I was taken aback. She came close and held my hand, "I hope you like my living room. I did my own decorating."

"You certainly have talent..." I whispered.

She stood tall and placed her arms around my neck, "You handsome devil. Stole my heart and now I can see I've lost my boss." With a kiss she brought us together on the couch.

"What would you like to drink? Orange juice or something more exciting?" she asked as she stood.

"After that heavy lunch, I'll stick with orange juice."

She went behind the bar. "Is Bruce usually that direct?" I asked.

"Direct? I don't think so. But I could tell, he really wants you to join us."

After several minutes I asked, "Did you have to pick the oranges?"

"Oh you! It was frozen so...are you teasing me?" Patti sounded frustrated.

"Sorry, You hadn't said anything," I answered

She brought two glasses on a tray, sat one on an end table for me and took the other to her seat nearby. "Now, how about a toast?" Patti smiled.

I offered, "To Pasadena Savings, and may you prosper." I hadn't expected anything like that.

"Well. I'll toast our future." Patti raised her glass.

I responded, "To the future." We touched glasses and resumed a side by side position on the couch. I was so thirsty I drank most of my juice before looking at her. "Seeing you through the glass, I realized you are beautiful besides being sexy and talented. No wonder Bruce wants you around."

"You are a tease. You had to look through the glass..." She smiled.

"I'm not teasing, just uncomfortable. What about your husband? He could come home anytime. I suppose." *Better say it now.*

"He's a C.P.A. With Bruce's help he developed a successful practice. He has offices in Pasadena and San Marino, and owns an apartment between them. He rarely comes here and always calls first. He says both of us would pay much higher income taxes as individuals, so we remain married." Patti was tense while going through that explanation.

She continued, "I get the feeling that you are avoiding me, because I am too realistic. Yes, I'm crazy about you, and I hope you'll find me attractive."

"Attractive? Hell, you are every man's ideal. Fantastic body, beautiful smile and great personality, but best of all you are right here!"

Patti responded, "Now that's much better. I'll be more comfortable in my bedroom. Care to join me?" There was that sexy smile again.

Her long black pants fell to the floor as we were close to the bed. With her arms around my neck we ended on top of the bed as she was trying to unbuckle my pants.

After the loving, Patti stood and held my hand. "Your talent as a musician doesn't equal your power as a lover. That was the most thrilling, passionate experience I've ever had. Please, darling don't leave me. My whole life would be renewed with you." Her kiss was warm and loving. Her breasts pressed against my chest and made a lasting impression.

I held her close, "Beautiful one, I have a dream. I'll take you to New Orleans for a week. You'll be immersed in a totally different life style. Where love is the essence of everything they do." I kissed her gently.

"I'd love it. Let's make it happen." Patti stepped away.

Our farewells were brief. "I'll call Bruce next week. See ya' soon." I went home. *She must have put something in that juice. I can't remember a word I said. She thought the loving was great. Maybe I'll feel that way tomorrow.*

A few days latter I called their office, the receptionist put me through to Bruce. "Thanks again for taking time to talk with me, and that elegant lunch. I've decided to stay with my plan, to become a veterinarian. Thanks for your generous offer, but I'll do it my way."

"I'm sorry to hear that. I thought you were bright enough to understand our business. Guess I was wrong." Bruce hung up.

Later I talked to Patti. "I suppose Bruce told you about my decision."

"Yes, he's very disappointed. I am too, hope we can get together soon."

"With finals I'm locked in right now. I'll call you after that." I tried to sound sincere, but she sensed my feelings.

"I'm counting on that trip to New Orleans." Patti was pleading.

"I'm dreaming of it. See ya' soon."

My grandmother had a saying, Money can't buy happiness. Patti is bright and attractive, but I didn't see signs of happiness anywhere.

70

REPLY
RED CROSS LADY

Harry Wilson felt bypassed by all the activity at the Great Lakes Naval Training Center late in the summer of 1945. Germany had surrendered and this was the focal point of a buildup for an offensive in the South Pacific. He thought of himself as a piece of flotsam thrown out of an eddy in the river where he fished, quietly waiting on the side while the current rushed onward to the sea.

He volunteered to work with severely injured men who were recuperating in the hospital, but not ready for physical therapy. This Tuesday afternoon, after a particularly difficult morning, he was emotionally drained and recovering in the Red Cross staff lounge.

A woman entered through the door from the hospital wing and by the smock she wore he knew she was a Red Cross volunteer. Without looking at Harry, she slumped into a chair opposite him. Crossing her arms on the faded yellow formica table top, she buried her face in the crook of her right elbow and began to cry softly.   Then, as a sob rocked her body, she murmured..."Oh no, it couldn't be."

As Harry pulled his chair beside her, he noticed her beautiful deep chestnut hair, shining like burnished copper where the light caught it. A mystical quality was created where it touched the deli-cate white flesh of her arm. He spoke in low gentle tones, "We all go through tough times, whatever it is it'll be better for you to talk about it."

Her sobs were subsiding, then intermixed with crying, they became soft sighs. Harry studied her hand and long slender fingers, each fingernail perfectly manicured with a natural polish. *She doesn't wash dishes and mop floors, more like an artist,* he said to himself.

Harry continued speaking, although she hadn't given any indication that she was listening. "You've got real troubles. My father had a saying, 'Cheer up! Things could get worse.' So I cheered up, and sure enough, things got worse."

Harry thought, *She might be in shock,* but he continued. "Father was a man who knew a lot about troubles. He homesteaded on the most bleak, desolate land in Southeast Montana. Indians, rattlesnakes and coyotes had left long ago. Our Government wanted farmers to raise beans, so they promised to pay half the cost of seed-beans, and guaranteed a price for every sack produced the following spring."

She is a new volunteer, Harry reasoned, for he knew all of the regular women. None of them looked as good in a smock as this lady. He hadn't seen shapely legs like this before.

He resumed, "The harvest didn't even pay for his part of the seed bill."

Pushing his cup out of the way, Harry leaned forward, "Lovely lady, would you have some of the Navy mud that passes for coffee in this place?" Even though she didn't reply, he got up, found a clean mug, then drained the last of the coffee into it and sat it in front of her. "I'm sure the Navy has a barge in the flats of Lake Michigan to suck up this muck and it's mixed with last week's grounds. The only way they could produce such a foul smelling brew."

Her head barely lifted as her fingers grasped the mug. She brought it close and started to take a sip, then shoved it away and resumed sobbing.

"You might think my Father learned a lesson with the beans, but not him. Next year, the Government wanted wild Mustangs that had been 'green-broke." My Father and two friends spent most of the summer to get ten horses ready for the Army buyer. Only three of their horses qualified, which didn't even make expenses."

Without raising her head from her arm, she glanced up at him through long lashes, "What are you talking about?" Mascara smudged black on a tear stained cheek, a gasp followed her question.

"Troubles," Harry said. "It seems like you have some kind of problem. Since you weren't doing much talking, I just wanted you to know I'm here, ready and willing to share and listen."

What he'd seen of her face fit the image he'd formed. *She's a beautiful lady of means, delicate and possibly a volunteer who encountered one of the most severely wounded men in this wing.*

She buried her face deeper in the curve of her arm.

Harry resumed after a few seconds, "I'm sorry the lady didn't care for the cafe-supreme offered by our new chef. Perhaps madam would prefer a few drops of the very special reserve which my Scottish grandfather developed. It's the 'drippins' that comes from the last of the mash used to make very good Scotch. I always keep a little wherever I am in case of a rattlesnake bite. Oh, you say there hasn't been a rattler around Great Lakes for years. Right, I say, but one could come on the next ship." He dumped her Navy Mud and from the storage space under the sink, brought up a brown glass bottle labeled "Poison." He poured a few drops of clear white liquid into her cup.

He moved his chair close to her, took her cold hand and placed it on the mug. "Lovely lady, sip this as though it was a delicate nectar. Just let a drop or two linger on your tongue before you swallow."

She stopped sobbing and seemed to compose herself. Without looking at him she slowly took the mug and sat upright, brought the mug to her lips and, as he'd suggested, sipped and held the liquid in her mouth then let it go down.

Harry took note of her light skin which reminded him of English porcelain. He noticed her chin, determined and stubborn.

After she sipped again, she sat back in her chair and turned to face him, "What was that you were talking about, beans and mustangs? You're crazy."

"That's what I'm trying to convince the Navy shrink. If I'm bad enough to be ruled incapable of performing my duties, but not so crazy that I have to be confined, I'll get an honorable discharge." He saw that she didn't think that was funny.

There was just a trace of a smile at the corner of her lips, "Your Grandfather must have been quite a man to give you his recipe for this nectar of the gods. I'll have some more." She moved her mug toward him.

Harry smiled, "Lady, you would have loved my Grandpa, and he would have told you that to sip a few drops makes the day bright, but to drink a little brings misery for the entire night."

He poured a little more than the first time and returned with the mug to sit beside her. "I'm sure that Grandpa would insist on introductions when a beautiful lady is enjoying some of his private liquor."

"To Grandpa." She raised her mug in a toast, "I'm Roxanne, recently inducted volunteer."

He noticed the diamond mounted in gold on her wedding finger, and now he caught the name tag on her blouse, Mrs. Andrews. "Is there a mister?" Harry asked.

"David and I were married two and a half years ago, after he completed Officers Candidate School in Colorado. He's gung-ho-Navy, all the way. He volunteered for Intelligence and went to Annapolis."

"Not often we see an officer's wife as a volunteer." Harry added.

"Soon after he completed training he was put in charge of a group for some super-secret thing. I don't know what it is, and he hasn't written or called for fourteen months." Her voice faded with the last words.

Harry reacted, "Wow! That's enough to break the strongest person. When will all this end?"

Roxanne motioned for a refill of her mug. "Officially, the only information I get is that he is alive, and engaged in 'Operation Zygote', which will affect the National Security. He is not permitted to contact anyone outside the project, and I'm not to try to contact him...for his own safety." She paused and sipped some liquid from her mug.

Harry wondered, "Unofficially, what have you heard?"

"Rumors. The Navy, especially officers' wives, thrives on rumors. The one consistent rumor is they are developing some super-bomb, powerful enough to end the war."

Harry leaned back in his chair, "Yeah, I have heard that one, and I'd be the last swabbie to hear the truth about anything more important than changing the chow schedule."

"Swabbie?" Roxanne raised a questioning eye. "I've never learned about the things on your sleeve. There are so many and they look alike to me."

He turned his left shoulder so she could see it, "Petty officer third class, Specialist X." He ran his finger over the lines. "My last name is Wilson, which is what they use in the Navy. I'd like to be called Harry."

"Harry?" She slowly rolled the 'r's, she pronounced it like a Scotsman. "I like it, and I'll take a little more of Grandpa's wonderful elixir."

Harry sat the bottle in front of her.

She poured a stiff drink without looking at him. "Harry." She paused, seeming to think about what she wanted to say. "Is there a Mrs. Wilson?"

"No. I've been so busy teaching and coaching I haven't had time for dating. In a small town if I took a girl out for a second date, the townspeople would have us married."

She responded, "You don't fit my idea of a sailor. You didn't have to do a thing about the neurotic volunteer who came into your room to shed a tear. How come?"

"A year ago I got a personal letter from President Roosevelt inviting me to help win the war. Who could resist an invitation like that? When I got here they didn't know what to do with me..." Harry paused, to reflect on what he'd said.

"Go on, I'm listening," Roxanne prompted him.

"They wanted me to be an officer. When I learned that the commitment was for life, and I could be recalled at the convenience of the Navy, I declined their kind invitation. They didn't like my attitude. Because I have a master's degree and had been a high school coach, they made me Specialist X, so they can assign me anywhere."

She thought a moment before offering, "Harry, I get the feeling that you are less than enthusiastic about the Navy. Did you really like being a coach?"

"I loved seeing immature boys develop into responsible young men. Working together, they learn to give up personal glory for the good of the team."

Roxanne finished the pint of Grandpa's special gift to mankind, and when she was sufficiently relaxed, Harry asked the question he'd been pondering since she came in. "Lady Roxanne, what was it that had you so upset?"

She gave a perceptive smile in recognition of his use of lady. "Swabbie Harry, I've only been to this hospital two times, once for training with a staff member and today to go into a ward to assist a nurse." Harry watched her tip the empty bottle and put it down. "The nurse gave me a writing pad and pen, told me the man in Bay D wanted to send a letter home. When I opened the door to his room, the position of his head on the pillow, short black hair and the shoulders...I was sure it was David. I flung myself on his neck and..."

Harry interjected, "It was someone else...how bad was he? Some in that ward are basket cases." He meant to sound sympathetic, but it didn't come out that way.

She turned away and began to sob.

Harry waited quietly for her to stop crying.

Without lifting her head, she slowly got it out. "The other side... of his face...was gone. No eye, just bandages down to the neck bone." Those final words tumbled out.

Harry softly offered, "These Navy Docs work miracles, rebuilding bodies all shot to hell."

Roxanne shuddered and looked at Harry, "It wasn't David, this time. But, maybe it's a premonition that David will come home looking like that?"

Harry reached, to lay his hand on her wrist, "I don't believe in that stuff, but there are many in this hospital that will tell you they had a vision or a message about the thing that happened to them."

She started to stand, but her knees gave way and she fell part way to the floor. Harry caught her and got his hands under her arms and pulled her back into the chair. She slouched to the back of the chair and with a glazed look at Harry said, "I can't make it."

Harry got a towel, soaked it in cold water then rubbed her hands, temples and forehead. "If you are going to faint, you couldn't have picked a better place." Gradually she revived.

She looked at her watch, "It's four o'clock. I ought to go home."

"Where is home?" Harry asked.

"An apartment, Northshore." She replied.

Harry quickly answered, "You can stay on the base."

She was speaking normally, "I hate B.O.Q., so sterile and un-friendly. I need to be in my own bed, my own home." Tears were in her voice.

He paused, then queried, "And how do you plan to get there?"

She answered, "My car. I've had some weird drivers from that motor pool."

Harry recalled the classic advice from his Chief, "Keep your nose clean, never volunteer and you'll get along." She looked at him, big brown eyes pleading for help,

"Harry, would you drive me home. I really shouldn't try it."

Harry thought, *Like that personal letter from the President that got me here, I couldn't resist a beautiful lady who loves my Grandpa.*

When Harry saw her big, white Cadillac, he knew he was in trouble. An enlisted man with an officer's wife was a major offense, subject to disciplinary action. To drive through the main gate in a car which was not part of the Navy Motor Pool would be another violation.

Usually there was a Marine guard at the gate, but fortunately it was a pea-green, smooth-faced farm boy in the uniform of the Navy Shore Patrol. Roxanne charmed him, "Yes officer, I know about the motor pool, but I need to drive my own car for medical reasons, see I've been to the hospital."

"Mam, you should have one of the Navy drivers..."

"Officer, he is an attendant at the hospital who understands my problems."

Out of frustration, and because there was a line of cars behind them, the S.P. waved them through. Harry saw a Marine sergeant in the Control Room writing, Harry thought, *Her license plate numbers, no doubt.*

Her apartment was in a building that had been converted from a Victorian of earlier years on a parkway north of Chicago, facing Lake Michigan. There were two units each on the ground and second floor, but she had the entire third floor to herself.

Large windows provided a magnificent view of the lake. A thick shag carpet, almost white, covered the floor, and her furniture was in bright colors, with chrome trim. Art work covered the walls, paintings by contemporary artists, framed prints of European scenes, and two large hangings of textured weaving in abstract designs.

Roxanne headed for her bedroom and told Harry, "Make yourself at home. Fix a drink if you want, but none for me."

Harry gazed out the window, then studied the pictures, trying to tune in to the person who created this environment. The empty easel in the studio and absence of any painting with her name intrigued him. He wondered, *Where are the personal things? Her wedding pictures and something to remind her of David?*

As she returned to the living room, Harry stepped back to see her. Her hair had been brushed, the mascara was repaired, and she moved gracefully in a full length green gown. He thought it was light blue until she stood in the light. Her eyes were lighted with energy and her smile conveyed a feeling of self-confidence which was new to him. She opened her arms, inviting him to come close. When he did, she put her arms around his neck, raised up and kissed him. "You saved me from a deep abyss. I'd have gone over the edge but for your caring help. You are wonderful!"

Harry remarked, "You are so beautiful, I'm at a loss for words."

They stood side by side, enjoying the moment and view. Harry offered, "It suits you fine. I get the feeling of the outdoors without having to be in the cold wind. You have enough space to do whatever you want without disturbing the neighbors."

Roxanne took his hand and led him to the tallest window. "I thought you'd enjoy the view. You impress me as one who spends a lot of time outdoors, alone." As she turned to look at him she choked on a sob.

He wanted to hold her close. "Yes, I am outside alone much of the time." He was tempted to let her know that he'd love to have her company.

She broke the spell and moved to the couch. "I could fix something to eat, but I'm afraid there's very little in the 'fridge."

"Thanks, but I need to get back to the base. I just wanted to make sure you've recovered, and can be here alone."

She replied, "My head hasn't caught up with my stomach, but that's from grandpa's elixir." She put her head on his shoulder and kept talking, but her speech was a combination of sobs and normal words. "I tried living on the base but couldn't stand the gossip and trivial things the other wives were doing."

Harry asked, "You moved here a few months ago and are you getting settled okay?"

Roxanne took a deep breath and spoke in even tones, "My shrink, I've been in analysis for almost a year, suggested I move out of the City and get back into painting and find some outlet for my energy." She paused and gathered her thoughts, "I've tried to paint and couldn't get started. Being a Red Cross volunteer was my way of finding an outlet for my energy."

Harry offered, "After today, you may want to find a different outlet."

"But, I wouldn't have met you." She kissed his cheek.

Harry took her hand, "Lady Roxanne, you are beautiful and a wonderful woman. You are everything I've ever dreamed of, and more, but you are married..."

She interrupted, "You have to remind me because I can't believe it's true."

Harry offered, "War does strange things. I'd never thought of being with a gorgeous woman in her fancy apartment. Forgive me if I don't know how to react. Give me a little time, and it'll work out for both of us."

She asked, "We will see each other again, won't we?"

"Of course, and soon." Harry concluded.

It was two blocks from her apartment to the "EL" station, so Harry was back in time for bed-check.

CHIEF DUMBROSKI

Harry respected Chief Gunners Mate Dumbroski. He knew ways to get things done that officers with layers of gold braid found impossible. When Harry asked a Yeoman, "How many years has the Chief been in the Navy?" he replied, "I don't know exactly, but the hash marks on his sleeve are for twenty years as Chief. He told me, 'before that I was just a stupid, ignorant swabbie. I'm not proud of what I did then."

The Chief took great pleasure in having a sailor with a Master's Degree in his command, especially one who turned to him for advice.

Harry had learned that when he wanted advice, it was best to bring a pint of Wild Turkey. After chow, with the bottle concealed in his waist band, Harry knocked on the door marked, "PRIVATE! Enter at the risk of your life."

"Chief, I've got a story to tell."

(For the sanctity of the home, the author has translated some of the Chief's vocabulary)

"Your stories turn into problems, unless I get you squared away in time." He was in his skivvies, sprawled on his cot listening to a news broadcast from London.

Harry had been here before. He discovered a dirty glass for himself and set the pint bottle on the floor by the Chief. Harry told him about the Red Cross volunteer who thought she saw her husband, a Navy Officer, in the ward. That her husband was assigned to Intelligence, Operation Zygote.

"Any way we could find out about him, and what's his chance of getting back alive?" Harry queried. With the two of them drinking, they almost killed the bottle while telling the story.

At first Harry thought the Chief was going to ignore him. Then he picked up the bottle and took a long drag.

"You stupid bleedin' asshole, haven't learned nothin' 'bout the Navy to come askin' that question. If I so much as raised the question, they'd send Special Forces out here so fast, you'd have lead in 'ur ass, 'n barnacles in 'ur mouth."

Harry wanted to know, "Have you heard what kind of super-secret project the Navy has that a smart, gung-ho officer might be on?"

Chief let Harry know that he wished he never heard that question, then took another swig. "Now, this here broad comes into the coffee shack where you been goin' daily, for some time, right?"

Harry shrank, "Yeah."

"She turns on the tear faucet and sings hearts 'n flowers. Right?"

"Yeah."

"What in the fukk'n hell is the wife of a junior officer doin' with a big car, 'n a fancy apartment on North shore?"

Harry gulped, "Seemed reasonable to me."

"Suppose she's legit? If her old man is assigned to some project, do you think the Navy jest let's her run around pickin' up enlisted men to take to her apartment?"

"Never thought of it that way." Harry mumbled.

"You stupid sunuv'a horin' muttha, ignorant swabbie. She'd have a guardian, phone tapped 'n anything goes in or out of that apartment is known and checked out. Whoever wants to know what he's doin, knows what she's doin'. They get her to get to him."

The only sound was the radio broadcast. Chief killed the bottle.

"Suppose somethin' else. Somebody wants information 'bout something or somebody here on the base, a smart college kid on Ships Company so he can move around without causin' suspicion looks like a soft touch. She might never ask you to get copies of a plan, just what seems like harmless poop that everyone knows."

"Oh-my-God." Harry put his hands over his face.

"After you are in love, you'll find any info they ask for."

Chief turned sideways on his cot, "Read the sign on my door, on your way out."

CAPTAIN'S MAST

Harry Wilson found his name at the bottom of a list of seven men to appear for Captain's Mast, Friday oh ten hundred hours. All were enlisted men assigned to Ships Company who had violated some section of the Navy Code of Conduct. Chief Dumbroski advised Harry, "Keep yur' goddam mouth shut. When the officer asks you for a reason, just say, 'No excuse, Sir.'"

"You mean I can't..." Harry tried.

"Dammit, I didn't say you can't. You say mor'n I told ya, 'n you'll rot in the brig."

A young Lieutenant J.G. was seated behind a desk, the U.S. and Navy flags displayed behind him. A bored yeoman had his old Royal typewriter on a small desk and a Shore Patrol served as bailiff.

Harry stood at attention facing the judge while the bailiff read: "Count One: Consorting with an Officer's Wife. Count Two: Driving an Unauthorized Vehicle. Count Three: Intimidating the S.P. Guard on the Main Gate."

It sounded to Harry that he was the most deceitful criminal to ever face the court.

"Specialist Third Class Wilson, you heard the charges, what have you to say for your conduct?" the judge asked.

Harry had to fight for control to say it. "No excuse, sir."

The judge studied Harry's face, mumbled to himself, then said, "You are sentenced as follows: Ten days in the brig. Seven days Prisoner At Large; confined to barracks and your duty station. Report to Chief Dumbroski every two hours, in uniform, and salute properly. The brig time will be suspended for the remainder of the calendar year. I'm warning you, any future misconduct will bring a Court Martial with the brig time automatically enforced."

Harry found the Chief, and told him the outcome of the trial. "You stupid knucklehead. He gave you a break. Suspended the brig time." He told Harry.

"What's he mean, barracks and duty station?" Harry asked.

"For Christ's sake, this here goddam building, 'n where you do whatever it is in the Hospital. It don't mean squattin' on yur' ass makin' out with wummin'."

"Every two hours for a week, I'm to report to you?" Harry asked.

"You mutha'fukkin idiot, you knock on my door after midnight, you ain't goin' to ever knock on any door agin. Report to the goddam guard 'n sign the log." The Chief was emphatic.

Harry snapped to attention and saluted, "Yes sir. Thank you, sir."

Chief responded, "That greasy assed shavetail will be on 'yur ass next inspection. You gotta learn how to salute. Get Yeoman Johnson to check you out.

Harry got an alarm clock and revised his schedule to be with patients during the one and half hour intervals between reporting to the guard. He slept in his uniform and allowed fifteen minutes to find the guard, so he could verify the signing of the log.

He longed for Roxanne, needed to call her and wanted to be with her. Tuesday he went into the wing where she had been, but didn't see her. He risked going to the lounge for a few minutes in the afternoon. She wasn't there.

Friday morning as Harry was preparing to leave for his 10:00 check-in, Mrs. Ferguson, Director of the Red Cross, took him aside. "She called, said it is urgent. Left these numbers and said you'd understand. Oh, I hope she's not in trouble, she is such a cheerful person, does us all good to have her around."

Harry looked to see if anyone was watching, "Thanks, I'm sure she's not in trouble. Remember, I'm not to be in touch with her, so keep this quiet, please."

Mrs. Ferguson smiled, "You're the finest enlisted helper we have. I'll be careful."

Harry decided to call Roxanne. She said, "There's a burly S.P. guard on the front door of my building. He requests I.D. from everyone going in and coming out. Another S.P. is outside walking around the building all the time..."

Harry responded, "Yeah. The enemy wants you, so they can get information from David. Sorry, your phone is probably tapped, and there may be a bug in your apartment. Just routine, the way the Navy looks at it."

Two days later Roxanne called while Harry was on the ward. She spoke as soon as he came to the phone, "Darling, I'll come to the hospital tomorrow afternoon. Let's meet in the lounge about 2:30, O.K.?"

Harry was surprised, but didn't want her to sense it, "Sure. Looking forward to seeing you."

It was a warm, sunny day so they walked in a grassy, enclosed area just outside the lounge. Roxanne wore the Red Cross wraparound which made her seem older than Harry, but he guessed she actually was one or two years younger. Harry gave her a warm hug, "Hello Darling, I've missed you, dreamed of you...well, us." They walked around the grassy area then sat with her back against a tree.

She replied, "Guess we may be sharing the same dreams." With Harry's head on her lap, looking up into her face, he said, "I want to hold you for as long as we shall live."

She kissed his forehead, "Darling, I'll love you and need you to hold and protect me as long as we live."

When they returned to the Lounge, a big M.P. with a .45 holstered on his left hip and a night stick in his right hand took Harry by the shoulder, and said, "Petty Officer Third Class, Wilson, your ten days in the Brig STARTS NOW!"

Roxanne burst into tears, "Oh No. You can't, I'm an officer's wife. I can't do without him!"

The M.P. and Harry exited the door from the Hospital and Harry was transported to the Navy Brig.

FALL OUT: HARRY

After serving ten days in the Brig for "Consorting with an Officer's Wife," Harry Wilson returned to his bunk in Outgoing Unit. The yeoman motioned for Harry to wait near his desk. "Pack your sea bag, with everything except a uniform, and Pea Coat. You will be leaving in the morning."

"Where to?" Harry asked.

The yeoman looked frustrated, "I don't know. Even if I did, I couldn't tell you. Chief Dumbroski wants to see you before you go, so be ready by 5:30 a.m."

The Chief was clean shaven, and in a fresh uniform. Harry was tempted to comment on his appearance, but the scowl on his face nullified that idea. "You mtha'fukuin knucklehead, supposed to be smart'rn hell, in all the years I been in the Navy, I never seen such a stupid, dumb-assed thing like you did. We had all the Security, Chicago Police plus a truck-load 'uv Fibbies (F.B.I.) runnin' inta each other, all lookin' fur you! Only thing missin, was the Methodists, cuz they wouldn't believe you'd be that stupid. "

"All the gold braid on this base was plannin' the court martial. They'd order a firin' squad 'n shoot you rather than take time away from the war to try yu'.

"You gotta get ur ass outa here 'fore them M.P's find ya'. Yoeman Swartz 'll take care, run like Hell!"

Harry was ready and his transport waited outside the door. It was a motorcycle with a husky man wearing a black leather jacket, goggles and helmet. He threw the sea bag over the handlebars. Harry sat on a small rack over the rear wheel.

Harry leaned into the back of the driver as they sped away. The driver waved to the guard on the Main Gate, and they were soon in Chicago traffic.

Their destination was the Navy field at the airport which is now O'Hare. Harry rode with cargo in a C54, four-engine plane, headed for California. Harry deplaned in Alameda, California, in a large airport with mountains of equipment, materiel and food headed for the South Pacific.

There were no signs to direct passengers. Eventually he found an office where he showed his travel orders to a young female 'Wave.'

"Where do I go, he asked?"

After she scanned his papers, "To San Pedro where you will be discharged." She returned to her work.

Harry rode a Greyhound Bus to San Pedro, and thought, "All the Gold Braid at Great Lakes, and F.B.I. lookin' for me, while I was in the Brig. Like they say, "If anything can go wrong, the Navy will see that it does.' Chief Dumbroski went way out on a limb for me. What a GUY! I ought to send him a gallon jug of Wild Turkey."

Harry took a cab to the Navy base, which exhausted his meager supply of money. He followed signs, "TO BE DISCHARGED." It was the smallest building in a large compound. A yeoman took his papers, wrote a note and attached it to the cover. In less than ten minutes, he became a CIVILIAN! It was three o'clock in the afternoon, he had back pay, a bonus for time served and wanted to find Roxanne.

FALL OUT: ROXANNE

When Roxanne returned to her apartment, Lt. Commander Overholtzer greeted her, "Mrs. Andrews, I have important news..."

She cut him off, "What are you doing in my apartment? Can't a lady have some privacy?"

He pulled himself up to his full five feet six inches, "I'm the officer in charge of security for all V.I.P.'s. Your husband is on assignment to a 'top secret' project. An enemy could take you hostage to get information from him..." She interrupted, "And the Navy makes an expendable chip out of me. Now, I must have some privacy in the bathroom." She strode across the living room, with him following, "leave me alone" as she closed the bathroom door.

He tried to talk through the door "There has been an accident..." but she flushed the toilet and he returned to the living room.

She took a few minutes in her dressing room before she came to face him. He repeated, "There has been an accident, your husband was injured. I'm here to assist you. You will fly to Hawaii, where he is being transported even as we speak..."

Roxanne interrupted, "The Navy plans my life, without so much as a question?"

The Commander was flustered, no one in the Navy would cut him off, and question a decision. "Mam, I will expedite your travel, so you can be with your husband. You are to leave within the hour from Chicago. You may be in Hawaii to meet the incoming flight bringing him."

Roxanne was accompanied by a gray-haired Catholic Chaplin, on a C254 twin-engine cargo plane. Temporary seats were bolted to the floor. It was spartan, but efficient. The motor noise prevented meaningful conversation.

They landed in Honolulu just after midnight and were rushed to the military wing of the Hospital. A nurse with insignia designating her as "Commander Jankowski, R.N." met them near the entrance, and asked them to sit down. She addressed the chaplain, "Father, perhaps you should take over."

He asked, "What can I do that you won't do?"

She turned to face Roxanne, "I have bad news to report. Would you prefer to be more private?"

Roxanne seemed to anticipate what was coming, "No, I can accept any news of my husband. I haven't heard from him for nearly fifteen months."

"There was an accident at the site where he has been stationed. Three fatalities, and two injured. Your husband was severely injured. He received first aid and was transported to the nearest air field. We were prepared to accept him, but were notified he died in transit. I'll assist you in any way possible, housing or whatever."

Roxanne held the hand of the chaplain and sobbed, then put her head on his shoulder. Soon they stood and he helped her to a restroom.

Father Joseph took Roxanne a short distance to an estate, the residence of the Bishop of the Catholic Church for Hawaii. His housekeeper welcomed her, and graciously asked Roxanne if she would like tea, or other refreshment.

Bishop McClarin greeted them and expressed sympathy over the loss of her husband. They were seated in a grand living room with religious paintings and figures arranged around the perimeter and on the walls. "My child," the bishop addressed Roxanne, "I want you to stay here, my housekeeper will fix a room for you and prepare refreshments as you wish. Sleep as late as you can, and we will help you anyway possible."

Roxanne was uncomfortable and spoke slowly, "I've never been in the presence of a bishop, so I hope I'm not impolite, but I'd like to ask a favor..."

"Speak up, my child. I'm human and understand most questions when presented in a spirit of seeking." The bishop responded.

Roxanne hesitated, then asked, "I'm a sinner. I haven't been to Mass for quite a while. Could you pray for my husband and serve the Sacraments to me?"

The Bishop shifted his considerable weight to lean forward toward Roxanne. He looked intently into her eyes, "With the help of Father Joseph, and your request for forgiveness, YES. We would welcome you into our Fellowship."

Roxanne was ushered into a colorful bedroom with scenes from the Outer Islands on the walls. She was sound asleep in a few minutes.

In the morning, before breakfast a courier delivered a heavy canvas pouch with "Reply C/O Red Cross" on the side.

In addition to the Church business, a letter addressed to Roxanne read, "Come to Philadelphia. Help prepare the funeral service for David. Stay with us as long as you can." Signed, Mr. and Mrs. Andrews.

Reply C\O Red Cross, Philadelphia.

FALL OUT: HARRY

August 15, 1945, Harry was in San Pedro, California, searching for a hotel. People came out of every building. They were shouting and singing, "The war's over! Japan surrendered!"

He cornered a sailor, "Is it true? Did they surrender?"

The swabbie was so happy, he grabbed Harry around the neck, and jumped up and down, "Sure as hell is!" The streets were jammed with celebrants, no cars or taxies dared try to get through. Harry continued in the direction he'd set, but it seemed hopeless.

Frustrated, exhausted and hungry, he found the YMCA Hotel. His call to Hawaii was finally transferred to the main switchboard of the Navy Hospital. "Sorry, sir there is no patient by that name here..."

In the lobby of the hotel, Harry met a sailor in uniform, Seaman First Class Jacobson. They struck up a friendship and went to celebrate together. Crowds were everywhere. They found "Sheepherders Shelter," with empty tables. Jacobson was from Minnesota. "My dad is a deputy sheriff, and proud that I volunteered."

Another sailor joined them. Machinist Mate First Class Micholson from Iowa. The trio had dinner, then headed across the street to a neighborhood bar. Micholson bought the first round, Jack Daniels straight. When they switched to beer, Harry bought a round. He hadn't gone to a bar since his freshman year in college. Later, he remembered the first pool game but blacked out after that.

After a shower, and a good night's rest in a real bed, Harry realized he needed a plan. With an objective. Get a job as a teacher? Take time to visit family and friends... search for Roxanne? He dug out the papers they gave him at the Discharge Desk and carefully read, "Inductees are entitled to counseling service, including determining career choice and placement service."

The desk clerk of the hotel helped Harry find a Red Cross Office. He sent a letter to Roxanne, in a big dispatch case, "I'm a CIVILIAN, please send a phone number so we can talk. C\O Red Cross, California. Love, Harry."

The next day, via Red Cross, three words survived the censor's knife, "Husband D.O.A. Honolulu Roxanne". It was in a dispatch case, Reply C\O Red Cross, Philadelphia.

September 21, 1945, in the Student Union of the University of Southern California, Roxanne found Harry for a reunion. She opened her arms for a hug, and Harry picked her up and swung her in a complete circle, "You are the most beautiful, wonderful woman on this planet! Best of all, we are together, and FREE!"

"You are the most handsome, wonderful man I could hope for. Yes, free of those Navy spooks. How did you manage to get a discharge?

Harry held her close, "We can talk for hours, catching up on the past. Let's go for lunch, where we can get a start."

Her kiss told him more than talking could. "I'm yours, forever." Holding hands, they walked a short block to 'Trojan Tommies' to find a quiet corner for lunch.

They rented a house in Palos Verdes with a 180-degree view of the Pacific Ocean. Harry was enrolled in studies leading to a Doctorate in Education. Roxanne applied for admission to the Cinematography Program at U.S.C.

Roxanne held her arms around Harry's neck, "Darling, let's get married in August next summer, honeymoon in Scotland, hoping to find Grandpa's Elixir."

Harry responded, "Will you go with me to pick out your engagement ring? You're the one who will wear it." "What a wonderful man. Yes, I'd love to." Roxanne kissed him lovingly.

FIFTH ANNIVERSARY

The morning after the party celebrating their fifth wedding anniversary Harry prepared a tray for Roxanne. Orange juice, a rose from her garden, coffee and a single slice of toast, marmalade, but no butter. As he brought it to her bedside stand, he sang a Scottish folk song, "Aye, it's nice to get up in the morrrning..." That's as far as he dared go.

"Mrs. Wilson, your tray is on the nightstand. You might try the coffee, it's your favorite brand." Harry tried to be cheerful.

Roxanne turned her face in his direction, "Lovely. Leave it and let me sleep a little longer," she mumbled, but he got her intention. "I'll take a walk and be back on an hour. Love you." NO response.

Two hours later, Harry took Roxanne out on the balcony of their Palos Verdes home which had become their favorite place to view the ocean and talk. She smiled and said, "That was very thoughtful of you, the tray with a rose was especially nice."

Harry responded, "My pleasure. That party was the most enjoyable I've ever attended. Our guests appreciated the view, and there were no problems which required action by the security officers.

"I thought Chief Dumbroski was particularly handsome in his new tailor-made dress uniform. Did you think the Chief and Mrs. Ferguson are a couple? They were holding hands as they left."

"I was too busy to notice." Roxanne said. "I couldn't get an address for either of them, so I used C/O Red Cross. I put two invitations in an envelope, took it to the Red Cross Office in Redondo and they assured me it would reach U.S.N.T.C., Great Lakes, IL, soon."

Harry asked, "Darling, what has been the most wonderful moment of these five years we have spent together?"

"That's easy. My wedding day. Our wedding, I should say...you were there." She smiled and kissed him on the cheek. "It exceeded my most extravagant dreams. The setting, on the country club lawn, allowed the guests to enjoy the view and the ceremony. The soloist, minister and even the flower girl did their parts perfectly. My only disappointment was that my mother couldn't make it. Dad died too soon, so neither were with me, except in spirit."

Harry brought her close and kissed her. "The most beautiful bride in all the world. And I loved you then almost as much as I love you now."

Roxanne waited a moment, "And the tall, handsome groom stole the show."

They paused and enjoyed the view. Harry wondered, "How about taking a walk to the beach?"

She slowly replied, "Walk down. Hike back up. No thanks! I was on my feet for two days preparing for the party, then yesterday was a very long day."

Harry wasn't going to be put off, "How about a soak in the hot tub?"

She showed some interest, "That's a good idea."

"Something to drink?" Harry asked.

Roxanne smiled, "I'll have Rosa make us eggnogs. You like them as well as her margaritas. Be there in a jiffy."

Harry waited in the tub on the deck, outside their master bedroom. As Roxanne approached in her "modest" swim suit, Harry whistled, then commented, "This is one of the greatest features of the house Roxanne built."

Roxanne slipped in and put her arms around his neck, then sat on his lap. "I hoped you'd like it." She paused and spoke in a more serious voice. "In a little more than a year, on my twenty-sixth birthday, I'll be responsible for the entire remainder in the trust which Grandpa Williams left for me. My CPA has urged me to request a full accounting for the history of the trust. The bank has been so generous and took a personal interest in my progress, that I'm reluctant. I'm sure that in due time, they will provide any report I ask for. How do you feel about it?"

"It was designed to provide for your education, which you got, and your first home, which we now share. It's entirely up to you. I'm glad to be with you here, but if we need to, we can get along just fine on our own." Harry relaxed and she moved off his lap.

"My financial planner estimates it may be a million or more. In any event, I need lots of help." She moved up on a ledge of the tub.

After a brief pause, Harry offered, "When I consoled a distraught officer's wife in the Red Cross Lounge, I didn't think I'd ever be in a hot tub with the producer of the 'Best Instructional Video of 1949.' What was that classification?"

Roxanne grinned, "For business and non-profit training purposes."

"Okay, the best of more than a hundred entries. I didn't know there were that many independent film producers in the country," Harry summarized.

Roxanne continued, "And I didn't think the only man in uniform who treated me like a human being would have mothers worshipping him like a... movie star."

Harry spoke, "I showed slides of boys five years, seven years and nine years hitting a baseball off a tee. The Physiology Lab at USC had movies made to show changes in development and hand-eye coordination. Those mothers hadn't seen anything like it. They loved it,"

"I've been giving workshops, lectures and demonstrations aimed at men and women who are coaching school and recreation teams when they have had no training and in many cases no experience in that sport. One of your videos would make it clearer and easier to understand than anything I could do."

"It made me realize there is a big market out there that we can tap into. All my handbooks are intended for coaches. But it's the parents who want to help their own kid who needs my material. What a great revelation!" Harry was really excited.

Roxanne picked up on his feelings, "It has unlimited possibilities. Right now I'm completing this year's biggest contract. I have two others to be fulfilled, so see me in my office before the end of the year." She was grinning from ear to ear.

Harry paused to think, "I need a vacation. More than a week, so I'll go backpacking in the Yosemite high country. How does that sound?"

"You are crazy. Remember I said that when we first met. We are in our best productive years, you can hike as much as you like later." She sounded a bit perturbed.

"Speaking of our productive years, when will we have time to …" Harry sucked in a fresh breath.

"Don't go there now. I'll select a time when I can stop working. I want to become a full-time mother when I have a child. No other productions." Her firm manner ended further talk about a family now.

Harry knew when to surrender. "Okay, okay. We will have five more wonderful years, working without a plan."

Harry queried, "Can we go out to dinner tonight?"

She said, "Yes, I forgot to tell Rosa what to prepare, so, that'll work."

"C" FOR COURAGE

PARIS FRANCE

"Dr. Wallace, there is a call for you from the States. Please wait in the lobby while I make the connections. You can take it in the booth nearby." The concierge who ran the switchboard served as clerk, bell-hop and general guide to American tourists. He was a tall, skinny Frenchman with long curly black hair.

My wife Alice and our daughter, Lindy, went upstairs to our room. In the Wallace family an overseas call would only come in an emergency, like a serious illness or a death. I thought of my father-in-law who retired and moved to Whittier two years earlier. To say he was overweight was too polite.

As I picked up the receiver I wondered, *Was it our eldest, Diane? The house? Chris?*

"Operator 86?" I asked.

"Oui, M'sieur. Speak English."

After clickings and static, Diane's voice came through. "Dad."

The booth was too small for my six-foot frame, so I left the door open and stood partially outside. It was hard to hear and difficult to recognize her voice, possibly because of the tension.

I responded, "Hi, honey...what is it?"

"I've got bad news..." She replied.

"About you?" A year earlier she called from Flagstaff, Arizona, at 4:00 a.m. There'd been an auto accident, she had minor injuries then, but she sounded much worse this time.

"No, Chris…she was in an auto accident on the Ventura Freeway. She was coming home from the camp for Junior Blind in Malibu Canyon. Oh Daddy! It was awful."

I could visualize Diane, who was usually calm in a crisis, bringing her hands over her face trying to wipe away the sight of her injured sister.

"Is she alive?" I wanted to know.

Diane replied, voice trembling and interrupted by sobs, "When the head doctor of the hospital (sob) called and I asked him, 'Is she alive?' (sob) he didn't reply, I repeated, 'Is she alive?' I raised my voice and shouted, 'IS SHE ALIVE?' Finally the doctor answered in a monotone, 'She's alive, but probably won't be by the time you get here.'"

Diane continued, "I screamed, She's my sister. She can't die."

Diane struggled to say, "Grandpa and Grandmother Atkins drove me out there. After one quick look, Grandmother Atkins nearly fainted and went back to their car."

I tried to console her, "That sounds awful. But she has family…"

She interrupted, "They haven't cleaned her, just stuck those needles into her for the blood and liquid that drops so slowly into her body." She paused to breathe.

"Yes, she's in a coma…" Followed by a big sob.

"Coma? Hospital in the Valley? Good God! How'd it happen?" I asked.

"They hit head on… the freeway is under construction." Her voice was getting close to normal, and she seemed in control.

"Was it Chris's fault?" I asked.

"No. She was on her side of the center line."

"How bad is Chris?" I thought of her as she was when I visited the summer camp a year ago, she helped blind kids learn to ride horseback and got them to handle barnyard animals.

"The doctor didn't want to move her more than necessary for emergency stuff, but I can see that the left side of her face and shoulder is mangled, and her left foot was crushed. Oh Daddy, it's terrible! The engine came right into Chris's side… even if she lives…" Her voice trailed off as she sobbed.

94

"If she lives?" I asked. "She has so much to live for, she has to live." I was forceful and affirmative, hoping to get Diane to feel likewise.

"I sure hope so..." Diane murmured.

"Anyone else hurt?" I wondered.

"Yes, the driver's wife was thrown out of the car and was struck by another vehicle. She was killed." Diane offered.

"Oh my God." My instinctive response.

"And one of his two sons was critically injured, the other had a fractured arm." Diane's voice was subdued, she barely spoke with enough force to be understood.

"What's the doctor say?" I hoped there would be something optimistic.

"That as long as she's alive, there is a chance that she'll recover. But Daddy, even if she does, she can't ever..." Her sobs drowned out anything else she said.

I waited a moment to collect my thoughts. "Have you contacted Dr. Bruff?" He was our family physician and personal friend.

"Yes, but he can't do anything while she is in that hospital." Diane whispered.

"How about car insurance, the Auto Club, we have our policy with them?" My thoughts were spinning about; how to get home to help care for Chris, what's the legal requirement? My little health plan will never cover the costs of this one.

Diane's voice was clear and natural, "Yes, the Auto Club is being helpful." Every phrase carried the horror of the crash.

"How about you? Are you okay? Anything I can do for you from here?" Trying to get her to talk about something else.

"ME? I hope I'll never have to go through another two days like this. Daddy, she's dead, except for those tubes putting God knows what kind of blood into her...then, I couldn't reach you. They only knew you were in Paris. NO! I never want to do this again." Then tears flowed..."I'm okay. I just wish..."

"We'll get home just as soon as possible. I'll call you tomorrow. Let's see, the time difference...it'll be about noon, your time. You're at home?"

"Yes."

"Love you honey. Sure am proud of the way you're handling things. Bye for now."

FAMILY MATTERS

As I climbed the spiral stairs to our second floor room, I thought, why did this happen to Chris? She has worked so hard, and has her heart set on becoming a veterinarian, just one more year at Cal Poly… What will Lindy want to do?

She could finish the program in Europe, or go home with us.

I found Alice nervously perched on the side of our bed. She stood as I entered. "What's happened?" I sat beside her and held her hand.

"Diane called," I tried to think of a way to tell her to minimize the shock, "She was being brave, but she had to tell us that last Saturday Chris was in an auto accident, heading home from Malibu Canyon…"

"How bad is it?" She had to know.

"She's in a coma. In San Fernando Valley. I believe Diane was still in shock. Her description was so vivid, she could hardly get the words out…"

Alice interrupted, "Alive. Thank God. I was sure someone had died, maybe Dad. How bad is she?"

Let's get Lindy in here, she'll want to know and then make her own decision. Okay?" I asked.

"Yes, certainly." Alice's tears were flowing.

Lindy, our fifteen-year-old, was waiting outside the door. "Come in honey. We have bad news and need to make some decisions." I stood and held her hand.

"Is it Grandpa? I heard the call was from the States." Lindy asked.

"No, It's Christine. She was returning from Malibu, must have been hit head-on. Let's get inside with Alice, to hear the rest."

"Chris? Why her? She's worked harder than the rest of us, and deserved the best."

Alice hugged Lindy and both sniffled and tried to hold back their tears.

"We'll have to get back home as soon as possible." Alice blurted.

The three of us sat on a too small bed that sagged with the weight. "Diane has done a fantastic job of getting the Auto Club and others to help. All I know is that Chris is badly injured, all the left side is damaged. The doctor did only the minimum necessary to handle the emergency. Serious head and upper chest damage, and her left foot was cut." I couldn't believe how calm Alice was, through all of this. Then I realized that this wasn't as bad as she expected.

Alice asked softly, "How was Diane standing the strain?"

"She sounded okay, but she might have been in shock." I tried to be reassuring.

"Where, how did it happen?" Lindy asked.

"On a section of the Ventura Freeway that was under construction. Chris was on her side of the center line, so it wasn't her fault." I reported.

I tried to be optimistic, "As long as she is alive, there is some chance of recovery. She is getting oxygen and blood transfusions so if she shows signs of coming out of the coma, they can examine her and begin repairing the damage." I sounded more confident than I really felt, how could anyone recover from such complete destruction of most of their body?

Alice sobbed and tears were on her cheeks. I suggested, "Let's hold each other, and give a prayer for Chris. I'm sure she can feel it, even if she can't hear us."

Each prayed silently, then together "Our Father which art in Heaven..." came naturally to a family that had attended church regularly.

"Lindy, we'll be going home to be with Chris, so you can either stay in Europe and finish the program, or come home... you don't have to decide at once, we have to find a flight and make the arrangements."

"I know what I want. To be with my sister!" Tear stained cheeks, lips quivering, she left no doubt.

I called Elizabeth. She was the tall, young Swiss woman hired by the Foreign Language League to coordinate the part of the program based in Switzerland. She was a university graduate and fluent in several languages. She had remarkable human relations skills and great insight into the needs of our students.

The entire school made the trip to Paris. We were housed in four hotels, distributed about the city. It took several phone calls to locate her.

"Oh Dr. Wallace, how terrible. What do you want to do?" she asked.

"My wife and I should go home as soon as possible. The concierge found that the first flight to New York is late in the day, tomorrow."

Elizabeth asked, "What about Lindy?"

"She wants to go home…but I told her to wait 'till tomorrow, she might change her mind."

"I'll call Headquarters in Salt Lake City, and get in touch with our Paris staff. We'll do everything we can to help. Call your home, or the hospital, whatever you need and charge it to the League." I wasn't expecting this sympathetic and helpful response.

Late at night, I had second thoughts. Alice sat up in bed and tried to control her sobs. I asked "What about our responsibility to the girls and their families?"

I was contacted by one of the partners who owned the Foreign Language League. He asked me to be a Consultant for the summer. All expenses paid and an honorarium at the end. Alice recruited six girls, including Lindy, so her expenses were paid. We were housed in Leysin, Switzerland, one of four schools throughout Europe.

Sobbing and gasping for breath, Alice was able to say, "Mothers would know that I have to go home, anything to help Chris."

"If you had recruited my daughter for an eight-week program, then left her with some unknown person… I'd be mad as hell!"

Alice responded, "We can talk with the girls in the morning…"

"Yeah. But that isn't like talking to the parents."

"You could call each of the families." I caught the difference, this was a "you."

"Let's give it some thought and decide in the morning." I turned my back and tried to get some sleep.

In the morning, the girls Alice recruited came by and each assured her that they understood, her first responsibility was to Chris. "Don't hesitate, go home as soon as you can."

Elizabeth brought a young Frenchman who represented the League in Paris and together they offered to make flight arrangements and take care of any other details. However, Air France reported the only flight that day was full and had a waiting list.

Elizabeth got through to Headquarters in Salt Lake City USA. They must have used some influence with the Consular Service and obtained one seat on the flight to New York, which the League paid for.

We made the decision, Alice would go home. Elizabeth drove her to the airport and stayed to be certain she was safely aboard.

I tried to sort out my feelings, shock that Chris was in an auto accident. She was a very careful driver, had a wonderful career mapped out and the future seemed to be in her control. I was proud of the way Diane handled a major crisis. Alice and Lindy will pull together and whatever can be done, will happen.

Lindy and I went with the other students and counselors to our home away from home, Leysin, Switzerland.

Three days later Alice called. Her father drove her out to the hospital in San Fernando. Her sobbing conveyed more than the words. "It's a miserable, terrible hospital. They haven't done a thing to clean her. No nurse is on duty…"

Diane stayed overnight, next to Chris since there was no nurse on duty at night.

I knew I couldn't help from here. I urged her, "Please, call Dr. Bruff. If anyone can help, he'll find a way."

LEYSIN SWITZERLAND

It was two days later when Alice made her first phone call, in time for dinner at the school. We were housed in a multi-storied building that had been designed as a sanatorium for TB patients. Leysin is a small village, clinging to a steep mountainside above Lake Geneva.

Her greeting was normal, "Hi Chuck. Diane met me and we went directly to the hospital. No matter how much she'd tried to prepare me, I couldn't bear to stay in the room after I saw Chris..." Alice struggled to control her voice, sobbing between words and crying at the end.

I asked, "You saw her? She's still alive?" Through the long hours since Diane's first call, I tried to keep a positive attitude. Now, with Alice's report... could I keep it up?

Alice continued, "She's worse than I'd thought. Can't see much with the tubes and equipment around her. All of her left side is mangled, they haven't tried to clean her. Clotted blood covers most of her face and the jaw bone is bared... I can't..." Static and sobbing were all that came through.

I offered, "Talk with Jim Bruff, see if he can take over. I'd feel much better if he was in charge."

Alice managed to reply, "I'll have to stay home tomorrow, so I'll try."

The best I could do was,"Keep believing that she'll get better. Call me tomorrow, about the same time. Love you, I'm praying for Chris and you."

"I'll do the best I can. Call you tomorrow."

As I returned to the dining room, I offered,"Lord, what does this mean?" I tried to get the message, but only felt lonely and disheartened because my family was separated during this crisis.

I never knew time could be so heavy. Twenty-four hours 'till the next phone call. I felt helpless. Sleep was impossible. First I saw Chris as a two-month-old baby when we moved from California to Madison, Wisconsin, so Alice and the girls could be with her parents.

Our train stopped just before crossing the Mississippi because of flood waters. A night in the cold, no heat and no food. After a long, hard trip by bus around the flooded area, we finally got to Madison.

After fitful sleep, I remembered when Chris was a freshman at Cal Poly University, San Luis Obispo, majoring in animal husbandry. Her calf won Reserve Champion in the Spring Poly Royal. Months of grooming, special feeding and hours of handling paid off. She had never been in 4H or F.F.A. and now she competed against the best in California. I was so proud of her it was difficult to refrain from standing and shouting, "She's my daughter!"

The counselors were helpful. Alice had recruited six girls, and two more were added so her way was free. I remained responsible for our Whittier girls, including Lindy. The other two went with counselors who had fewer than eight.

Students attended classes in French from 9:00 a.m. 'till noon. Afternoons were to be planned by the teachers and counselors. Most afternoons I managed to get back in the office in hopes Alice would call between 5:00 and 6:00 p.m., dinner hour for the students.

I took the phone on the first ring, "Hello Alice, how are you holding up?"

Her voice was weak, "I haven't been able to sleep. I did manage to eat a little, so I'm starting to get back to normal. I didn't go to the hospital today, called twice to hear their impersonal response, 'no change." She sounded all worn out.

"Lindy wants to talk with you, she's waiting. Anything urgent that I should know?"

"Lindy? No... I'll go to the hospital tomorrow and call about the same time. Bye, Love."

I left the room so Lindy had some privacy. She and Alice talked for several minutes. Lindy repeated her request to be with Chris.

Alice had responded that when Chris begins to recover and could have visitors we would do all we could to get Lindy home. Right now, there wasn't any point in it.

She learned that our friends, the Swensons, who live in the San Fernando Valley, offered their extra room so Alice could be closer to the hospital. She would move some of her things and go there tomorrow.

Lindy broke into tears as she told me, "I need to be with my sister, it's terrible not knowing, what she's like, what they are doing, just what is going on?"

I've never been good at calming a girl in tears, so I just put my arms around her and reassured her that we loved her and would do all we could for Chris.

Our room, which seemed much too large without Alice, had floor to ceiling sliding glass doors and windows which provided magnificent views of the Rhine Valley, amid majestic Alpine peaks. Somehow, that didn't help me get to sleep. I'd see Chris with all those tubes and monitoring devices surrounding her and in desperation I'd yank something loose just to see her.

I remembered when we took Chris to the dentist after she jammed her baby teeth into her upper gum. The doctor moved them back into place, and stitched the skin. After it was over, Chris in a very formal manner, said, "Thank you for taking good care of me." The doctor was amazed, after all that trauma for her to be able to say anything was remarkable, and for her to be so polite was most unusual.

All three girls loved animals, but Chris had some special feeling which she communicated to them. Her pet cats, dogs, guinea pigs or birds responded to her attention in ways which were different than for the rest of us. She kept them calm and rarely did one of her pets disappear.

We bought a small horse when Chris was nine, a Mustang with a splayed front leg. It was beautiful to watch Chris get on him, bareback. She had him under control with very little effort, and flowed with every movement of his body. We lived near Rolling Hills Estates, in Southern California, where many families kept beautiful registered Thoroughbreds or Arabians. Chris rode our Mustang in one of the local horse shows and won second place in the bareback competition! It wasn't just the ribbon, it was the fact she beat kids on beautiful registered horses who had years of expensive training.

Alice was distraught. From the moment I picked up the phone I could feel her struggling to remain in control of her emotions. "I've never been so mad in my entire life...that hospital doesn't give a damn about Chris!"

I'd never heard her so upset about anything. "What have they done?" The shock of hearing her got through.

"Nothing!" She blurted.

"Now be specific. Let's try to sort things out..."

"They won't put a nurse on Chris's case, so only the duty..." She lost control, and I just waited.

CHANGE

One week after the accident, when I picked up the phone, I had a feeling that things were better. Alice proved it true, "Hello darling."

I hadn't heard her so positive in a long time. "You'll never guess so let me tell you." I could hear the lift in her voice.

"Yesterday, the head of the Auto Club legal staff personally came in the morning to see what was going on at that hospital."

The Manager of the Whittier office wrote a memo to Wayne, so he took charge and came out there yesterday. In just a few minutes he was laying down the law to the doctor.

"Our patient gets the very best you can provide. There will be a full-time registered nurse on duty in the daytime and a duty nurse all night."

"The head of the enforcement division for the Medical Licensing State Office was a roommate of mine in Graduate School. He will hear from me in great detail and I promise you, there will never be another emergency patient in this dingy pretence of a hospital."

I broke in, "WOW! That is real service. How did the doctor take it?"

"He was in shock. First a bit defensive, but later he just listened."

"Wayne set some conditions. He'd come back by 12:30 and there would be a registered nurse on duty, with another employed for the evening. A stand-by nurse for the night shift is okay. Auto Club pays for everything if you keep good records."

"Did it work?" I couldn't believe the change.

"The first nurse is wonderful. She immediately cleaned Chris's face and covered some of the wounds with gauze soaked in saline solution. Her attitude is so different, she believes Chris will wake up soon. I'm to hold Chris's hand and tell her stories, any kind just so she hears my voice, and feels someone cares."

"Diane has been staying here all night. With the added nurse, she can go home."

"How wonderful! Tell Chris that the entire group of students in Leysin had a moment of silence for her before supper last night, and some will continue it 'till she is better."

The next evening when she called, Alice began speaking without a greeting, "A flood of calls have come from Cal Poly students and kids from the Foundation for the Junior Blind. Chris must feel that kind of support."

I felt so much better that I offered, "I guess I can stand it for another three days, if your next report is as good as this one."

Alice responded, "Hope it's even better. I got your two letters, thanks, it helps. Three days then, unless there is a change. Love You. Bye."

Two days later her call came at 5:00 p.m. "I thought you'd want to know. Yesterday, the hospital demanded cash up front for one week of the cost for the special nurses. That evening the Auto Club delivered a cashier's check by messenger and a copy of a letter to the California State Licensing Board, charging them with incompetence and failure to provide essential services."

My reaction was immediate, "WOW! How did the doctor react?"

"He hasn't said a word to me since then, but we have excellent nurses and the quality of bloods and plasma now is the level she should have had all the time."

"What do you mean?"

"I don't know the details, but Wayne did and insisted it be done for her."

Her call came at 5:00 p.m. two days later, "I've got good news!" Alice was elated.

"Good, I'm glad. Do you realize this is the thirteenth day since the accident? I need something encouraging."

"When I was telling Chris the names of her friends from Cal Poly who have called, I felt a response in her right hand."

"You did? That's fantastic!" I was beginning to feel some of the excitement which Alice displayed.

"An hour later I tried it with a nurse holding Chris's hand…"

"The one who's been so helpful?"

"No, a young girl just finishing her training. She wasn't certain, but agreed that something happened."

"How about your buddy, the doctor?"

"The nurse told him, and he just grunted, wouldn't come to see…until he did his rounds. Of course, by that time, nothing happened."

"Lindy is just outside the office, I'll let you tell her. Anything else I should know?"

"That's enough. Call you in three days. Love you."

When Alice told Lindy, her shriek was loud enough to be heard in the dining room.

The next evening at 5:00 p.m., Alice called. "I just had to tell you…"

"I'll take all the good news you can give." Her excitement came through loud and clear.

"Even that … ass, agreed, Chris responded by squeezing my right hand when I read the names of Cal Poly kids. The doctor measured it with electrodes on her skin, so he was convinced."

I interrupted, "How great! Does that mean she's on the road to recovery?"

"Barely. But, it's a lot better than it has been, and we can hope for progress, one day at a time."

"You sound much better. That's as good as your news about Chris. Have you told our friend and family doctor, Jim Bruff?"

"I ate a full meal for the first time, and took a nap this afternoon, so I'll do fine. I'll call Jim tomorrow."

The good news affected the entire Foreign Language League group. Smiling faces and friendly greetings became the norm.

Alice called the next evening. She was still elated, but her voice had a serious tone. "Chris responded three times this morning, so she is steadily improving. I called Jim Bruff, he had talked with the doctor here. Jim is too professional to say anything critical, but he recommended that Chris be moved to Presbyterian Hospital in Whittier, as soon as arrangements can be made." Her quavering voice conveyed Alice's feeling of insecurity.

"I take it, you have some doubt?"

"Yeah. The doctor says it is too dangerous. If I insist, I'll have to sign a waiver relieving him of all responsibility."

I reacted, "Responsibility? We can sue him from now 'till Hell freezes over. I'd go with whatever Jim Bruff recommends. Chris needs the best care we can provide, and that isn't in the hospital where she is now."

Alice, still uncertain, replied, "I hear you. I'll get back to Jim and tell him to complete the arrangements."

"Use your best judgment. Call the attorney from the Auto Club if you'd like some advice. Don't let that doctor intimidate you, since he's treated you so shabbily."

"I'll sleep on it, and take care of it in the morning."

"You've done so much, do what you think best. Please call tomorrow, Okay? Love you, bye."

MOVED

Alice's voice carried her grief across the miles of telephone lines. She hardly needed to say the words, "Chuck, we've lost her. The ambulance ride…too much."

I cut in, "Oh dear God. Why?" Tears that had been held back too long, streamed down my cheeks.

Lindy, felt the pain but took the phone from my hand, "Mom, What happened?"

"When the ambulance which carried her from San Fernando arrived at the Emergency Entrance of Presbyterian Hospital, Whittier, the attending medic told the doctor in charge, 'Sorry, we lost her a few minutes ago. The ride must have been too much for her."

"Dr. Jim Bruff told them, "Put her on the table. I know that girl. She has more courage than most of my patients. If anyone can make it, she will."

"He's still working on her... but."

That was the last Lindy heard.

She replaced the phone, then looked at me, "Dad, there's still a chance, I know there is." She sat beside me and we prayed in silence.

She spoke first, "Mom wants her to live, as much as you and I do."

I said, "But she felt that Chris was gone…" I was so dejected I couldn't think of anything else.

"Mom was so upset by all this that she couldn't see straight. Dr. Bruff is the one who knows best, and he's still working on her. That means there's a chance, and all Chris needs is a chance." Lindy sounded so positive, I felt she was just trying to keep my spirits up.

My response was, "If the Good Lord decided it was Chris's time…"

Lindy persisted, "Chris gets to decide. She wants to live, just as much as you or me."

"Lindy, you're wonderful and I love you dearly." I gave her a hug.

My room never seemed so lonely. Dark clouds sailed up the valley below, and even the mountain peaks were ominous. I recalled passages from the Bible that could have provided insight and solace, but nothing helped. Selected lines from classical literature came to mind, even descriptions from mythology about death and suffering were dug out of the past, all to no avail.

"Lord, Lord, help me understand. Life means so much to her, and it seems so little to ask for someone as wonderful as Chris. Please, let her live." I knelt at the foot of my bed as I prayed, and no answer came, that I heard.

Hours later, I was still looking out the windows hoping for an answer. There was a vigorous knock on my door. "Dr. Wallace, there's a call for you."

A masculine voice carried over the static. "Chuck, this is Jim Bruff."

"Jim, what's happened?"

"We got Christine on the table, she's …"

"You mean she's alive?" Still in shock from Alice's news, I wasn't sure I'd heard correctly.

"Yes. With a stronger pulse than when she left the valley."

"Thank God! Jim, we can't thank you enough. Once more you have done so much for our family."

"I gave Alice a sedative, but I wanted you to know as soon as we felt Chris was past the immediate crisis."

"Yeah, thanks so much for calling. From what Alice said, I'd given up. This is the greatest news. I remember when you were sailing through Organic Chemistry and took time to help me. That meant a lot to me."

"I never sailed through anything at Whittier College, glad I could be of help. Chris isn't out of danger, but she is where we can watch her, and I'll know she's getting good care."

Later that week they did the first surgery, on her mouth and left side of her face. Her recovery was so successful, they did the second surgery on her shoulder and left arm sooner than originally planned. Her ribs were taped and she had a back brace.

When we returned to California three weeks later, and made our first visit to the Whittier hospital, we were amazed to find Chris in a wheelchair, waiting to meet us in the Visitors Room. Her left arm was in a cast, taped to her chest with her hand near her throat. Her jaw was wired with a tiny opening to permit a straw through her lips.

"Chris!" Lindy ran to her and held her right arm, about the only available place.

Through all those bandages and braces, Chris's good eye sparkled and she drew Lindy close to her. Words couldn't express the love shared at that moment.

I moved as close as I could, bent down to absorb the thrill of seeing her alive. Feeling her good arm around me was reward enough.

The head nurse stood nearby, tears of joy came down her cheeks. She told of Chris's remarkable progress and what a pleasure it was to have her in the surgery recovery wing.

I was visiting one morning when Jim Bruff came on his rounds. He told Chris, "You saw the X-rays and know the extensive damage we will be repairing. You will have limited use of the leg, and the knee could fail at any time if you try to walk. You will be in a wheelchair, and probably never be able to walk."

Through the wires around her mouth, Chris replied "I WILL TOO!" The words weren't distinct, but the meaning was clear.

After fifteen surgeries, Chris was recovering in the surgery ward with one to eight other patients. Alice and I went to visit after supper. The wire guard around her mouth had been removed a week earlier, and this was the first time Chris felt like having a gab-fest.

Chris told us, "I missed a big date, Diane and I were to have a double date with Bob Howard and Chet Lewis the night of the accident. Bob is a Cal Poly graduate and was on campus the last week of finals. Somehow we met. He asked me to join him for a cup of coffee, and we went to Starbucks, talked for more than an hour. He called while I was in Malibu, and set up the double date.

"When I asked Diane, she wondered how I knew them? I told about meeting Bob at Poly, and Chet was a counselor at the camp for

Junior Blind. When I told her Chet is a black man and a really nice guy, she agreed."

I interrupted, "Is that as bad as not getting to go on your trip to Europe? And pick up a new M.G. to use while you go all over Britain?"

"Oh, that too." Chris laughed.

"By the way, I've cancelled all the reservations for hotels and 'B&B's. The travel agent said she was glad to do something for you."

"How about Kay Heinzer?" Her friend, Kay, was to go with her to London, and see Britain.

"Diane called her soon after the accident. Kay was disappointed about missing the trip but much more concerned about you and hoped for your recovery."

"Kay's father called to wish you a speedy recovery and offered to pay a share of any expenses related to the cancellation of the trip."

"I assured him there were none."

Every day more cards and letters arrived with wishes for a speedy and successful stay. Bob Howard provided a daily report on Chris's progress on a local radio station where he was a disk jockey. The audience, mostly teenage girls, had prayer groups, "good luck" parties and made their own get-well cards. Large boxes and huge cartons accumulated in the ward.

The next day, the Chief Physical Therapist for the hospital, Dr. Larry Thomas, came to see Chris, carrying two large folders. Looking at a file, he commented "You have made remarkable progress, keep that up and we will amaze the doctors with what you can do." Chris responded,"I'll swim and ride horseback. That will impress more than doctors."

Eventually she was allowed to come home. Walking in the house, from chair to table, she felt freedom at last. We started re-learning primary numbers, spelling common names and then the names of the states. Numbers one through five were easy, addition, subtraction and division came slowly.

She had been a strong swimmer before the accident, and was eager to get into the water. We started with her sitting on the edge of our pool, legs in the water, gradually lifting one foot at a time gaining strength every day, then adding weights attached to the bottom of her feet.

Getting up and sitting down was difficult at first.

She was strongly motivated, disappointment came frequently, but I never saw her give up or imply that it was too hard.

One afternoon while we were working on 7 times 8, Chris stated the formula for an organic compound. "I can't remember its name or if it was a fertilizer or food. I'm sure it was on the final exam in Organic Chemistry at Cal Poly."

I called, "Back to the hard work, what's 8 times 7?"

She made great progress on the leg exercises, soon she was standing in the shallow end and holding to the gutter. "Watch Dad, I'll make it across the end of the pool." Dr. Thomas was thrilled.

"I do wish you would finish your college education. Is it in your plans?" I asked her.

"I'll do it a little bit at a time. Chet and I want to get married."

In the spring of 1965, she told me that Chet, a black man, had asked her to marry him. She wanted to accept. "I have nothing against Chet, he's a fine young man. Certainly you realize it will require additional effort for both of you to keep an interracial marriage together. I know you can do it but it will be very hard."

Later, she enrolled at Cal Poly Pomona in two classes that would apply toward her graduation requirements.

After the second class session she broke down, the only time that happened in this whole process. "Dad, I just can't do it. I couldn't remember a thing from Monday class to Friday. I even studied two evenings on it. My memory just isn't good enough."

Chris and Chester Lewis were married, July 17, 1966, in the Chapel on the campus of Whittier College. A beautiful bride, wonderful ceremony and they got off to a good start.

On a fall afternoon I visited them. "Chris, how's it going? Marriage and living in a different neighborhood?"

"Chet and I get along fine. I'm having a tough time, as the only white person in an all black neighborhood. Just going to the market, I get called 'bitch' and yelled at to get out of 'our' town. One time in the market, two women each pushing a cart, blocked my passage and pushed me into a corner. Using profanity they called me a 'white whore, with a black brother. Go back where you belong." I pushed my way through them and left, without my groceries.

I offered, "Remember the old adage, 'sticks and stones will break my bones, but words will never hurt me." That's no fun but try to find a way to meet some of them on their turf, such as the church and see if that will break the ice. You are a foreigner, in their land. Try to avoid confrontation, verbal or physical."

"Dad, I try. There are times when it's impossible."

"You have shown so much courage and patience, I know you can do it, one more time."

In less than six months, their car was vandalized twice, leaving graffiti on the windows saying more of the same thing. Their apartment was broken into with valuables taken, including an expensive sound system which was Chet's pride and joy.

When Chris received the settlement from the insurance company, she and Chet looked for a house in an integrated neighborhood. They found a place in Altadena where Asians and families from Eastern Russia lived. Other couples of mixed races were accepted as well

In April 1973, Chris called with excitement in her voice, "We're pregnant! Those doctors said it couldn't be done, but with the help of the Clinic at U.C.L.A. it worked." Alice and I reacted together,"That's wonderful. Do you have an estimate of the due date?"

"I know more about that than the nurses, December of this year or January next year."

"Take care of yourself and we wish you well."

A baby girl, Carolyn, came six weeks early, December 24, 1977, and since Chris was RH negative, meaning there were deficiencies in the red cell production in her body which could adversely affect the baby, the doctors were very cautious about proper care for the child and mother.

Alice and I visited the evening of the birth and were told, "With the mother RH negative and all the transfusions she had, we will take the precaution of a complete exchange of blood for the baby. It's scheduled for 9:00 a.m. tomorrow. You can watch from the observation section, if you wish."

We were there early. A few minutes after nine o'clock, the head nurse told us, "Doctor tested her blood, and since the other vital signs were positive, he has postponed the blood exchange. We will put it on stand-by just in case it's needed. My guess is, that baby is healthy and won't need it." Which proved to be true.

Their second child, Craig, was born four years later with little trouble at birth. He has grown to be a large, strong young man.

2003 UPDATE

In December 2003, at an informal gathering of some of the Wallace family, I sat with Chris in a quiet corner and asked her, "What long-term effects of the accident you had when returning from the Camp for Junior Blind, have affected your life?"

"The loss of short-term memory is a constant reminder. Dr. Bruff said, 'There is nothing that medicine can do. The basal skull fracture damaged your brain, it doesn't repair itself, so you will have to adjust to it." Chris replied.

I picked up on that topic, "Which kept you from completing college, and meant you didn't become a veterinarian, right?"

"Yes, and in the animal hospitals where I worked, I know I would have been as good as many of them. There are a few outstanding doctors, and I couldn't hope to be that good." Chris was very serious.

I changed the topic, "And something about your fourth and fifth fingers on your left hand, correct?"

"There aren't any sensory nerve connections, so I can't feel hot or cold. Several times, while I'm cooking I've smelled something burning, looked down and it was my little finger, left hand." That's not funny.

"Those two fingers move together, so I can't play my flute." Her voice showed the disappointment. She had been the first chair flute player in the Pioneer High School band, which was where she had the most fun in high school.

Chris was a big girl, from early childhood through adult life, she was heavy. In July 2002 she joined Weight Watchers, and went on the prescribed diet. She also started a supervised exercise program. She lives near a canyon, surrounded by foothills. Her schedule started at 5:00 a.m. out the door, descend approximately 200 feet to the bottom of the canyon and hike to an elevation near 4,000 feet where there was a bench to rest and catch one's breath. Return home for hot tea and biscuit before going to work. The hike was eight miles, round trip. This was done four to five times a week. Once a week she attended a Weight Watchers check-in and had a pep talk, to stay on the program. By June 2003 she had lost 49 pounds and looked and felt like a new person.

In 1997, her husband Chet suffered a congestive heart failure. It took almost two years and at least three specialists to arrive at a diagnosis. The left ventricle muscle had deteriorated. He was placed on the list of those waiting for a heart transplant. He has remained on the list, although the muscle has improved slightly. Currently, he has a pacemaker and a defibrillator installed under the skin of his chest. He is a specialist in Workman's Compensation, and works as an independent contractor for insurance companies, as needed.

Carolyn age 29, graduated from high school. She had some photographs published in the school annual and was an outstanding player on their girls' softball team. She has studied photography and journalism at Pasadena City College. Currently she works in a photo shop nearby and takes care of the store when the owner is not there. She takes "informals" for wedding parties.

Craig, age 26, is a big man, taller than his dad and weighs more than 200 pounds. He played Little League baseball and was a member of the All City team for Pasadena. He graduated from high school and Pasadena City College. He has been a teacher in a private school established by parents from Jet Propulsion Laboratory and Cal Tech University. They have pupils "from diapers through grade six." The staff and pupils love him. He plans to complete the requirements for an Elementary Teaching Credential through California State College L.A. soon.

Christine has worked as a Veterinary Technician in animal hospitals for nearly twenty years. She has a wonderful way of relating to animals when they are under stress. Doctors frequently call her to come help get an injured pet to calm down for examination or treatment, even when the doctors and other assistants have tried.

The highlight for Chris in recent years was a trip to Ireland where she and a girlfriend went to a Horse Training School. They passed the required tests for riding and went on a five-day horseback ride in the Northern farmlands. No guide, just a penciled map and the names of farms where they stayed at night. To add to the excitement, they were in Dublin on September 11, 2001. No planes flew to the USA. A family in Dublin offered their home for the stranded Yanks.

Yes, there have been bumps along the way but as a proud father and grandfather, I find this a loving, caring family. They provide a wonderful example of how people who share a rich love can overcome adversity in any form.

WINTER BEAVERS

I live on a Nature Conservancy Preserve in Wisconsin with beaver ponds and active beavers. My favorite has been there for many years as attested by the gnawed stumps on each side of the dam going back several yards as each year the animals had to hunt further and further for food and dam materials. There is a big log far enough back from the dam where I can sit and observe their activities without disturbing them.

Last October we had a storm which left snow on the ground overnight, and I went to watch the beavers the next day. I sat on my favorite log and didn't see any movement in the pond. Soon I heard the clickity-click sounds of beavers talking.

It was the old Lady yakking at the old Man, "Here it is, the first winter storm and you haven't begun to gather the wood we need."

He may have answered, but I didn't hear anything.

She was at him a few minutes later, "You know we have to finish the room for the baby. You were the one who wanted Junior. Said there wasn't anyone to carry on the family... well, get out there and bring in some finishing willows".

Still no response.

"Just look downstream at the Jones's dam, all finished and a supply of winter wood.

You don't hear them talking about having to add a room, no siree. She said one baby is enough... all those sharp teeth. She won't go through that again."

Whatever he said was muffled by their swishing around inside the den.

"You heard me! Get out there and don't come back 'till you have enough willows to finish the room for the baby."

WHAP! She slapped the surface of the water, even from inside the den the sound was as loud as a deer rifle.

Old Mr. Beaver came out and surfaced near the dam, looked around and saw me so decided he couldn't come to this side to hunt for wood. He went upstream and into the Marsh on the far side. After a few minutes he came back without a single stick.

He swam around aimlessly, upstream then around the far side of the pond. Finally, he dove and went back to the entrance to his den. She had closed it. Locked him out!

"Clickity-clack (Beaver profanity no doubt) let me in or I'll never come back".

There was no response from inside the den.

He surfaced, WHAP! His shot was louder than the one she had given him and must have sent shock waves into the family living room. He went into the marsh, and hadn't returned by the time I left.

Two days later I saw a neat pile of willow branches, all stripped and ready for the winter on the far bank. It was more than a week before we had another storm that left snow on the ground so I guessed that peace had returned to the local Beaver family.

www.ingramcontent.com/pod-product-compliance
Lightning Source LLC
Chambersburg PA
CBHW051437280526
45785CB00003B/1319